The Fifth 200
Questions Answered
By Dr. D. A. Waite

I0138637

Real Questions From Real
People With Real Answers

Published by

THE BIBLE FOR TODAY PRESS

900 Park Avenue
Collingswood, New Jersey 08108
U.S.A.

Pastor D. A. Waite, Th.D., Ph.D.

𝕭𝖎𝖇𝖑𝖊 𝕱𝖔𝖗 𝕿𝖔𝖉𝖆𝖞 𝕭𝖆𝖕𝖙𝖎𝖘𝖙 𝕮𝖍𝖚𝖗𝖈𝖍

Church Phone: 856-854-4747
BFT Phone: 856-854-4452
Orders: 1-800-John 10:9
e-mail: BFT@BibleForToday.org
Website: www.BibleForToday.org
fax: 856-854-2464

We Use and Defend
The King James Bible

April, 2013
BFT 4014

Copyright, 2013
All Rights Reserved

ISBN #978-1-56848-085-5

Acknowledgments

I wish to acknowledge the assistance of the
following people:

• **Yvonne Sanborn Waite**--my wife, for
encouraging me to publish these questions
and answers, for reading the manuscript
carefully; for putting in various boxes; and
for giving other helpful suggestions for the
body of the book and the cover.

• **Julia Monaghan**—who volunteered to help with the
proofreading of the book, and had many suggestions for clarity,
as well as other helpful changes.

• **Anne Marie Noyle**–a faithful supporter of our
Bible For Today ministries and an attender via the Internet
of our **Bible For Today Baptist Church**, who read the
book and gave valuable suggestions.

FOREWORD

- **Thirteen Sections**. This is the fifth series of 200 questions that have been sent to me (## 801-1000). I have answered them as simply and as clearly as possible. The answers to questions ##1-200 can be found in **BFT #3309** @ **$12.00 + $7.00 S&H**. The answers to questions ##201-400 can be found in **BFT #3373** @ **$12.00 + $7.00 S&H**. The answers to questions ##401-600 can be found in **BFT #3482** @ **$12.00 + $7.00 S&H**. The answers to questions ##601-800 can be found in **BFT #3494** @ **$15.00 + $7.00 S&H**.

- **Some Of The Question Topics**. In this question and answer book, there are questions about the King James Bible, questions about the New Testament, questions about original Bible texts, questions about the Chinese Union Version (CUV), questions about the Greek New Testament, questions about the Hebrew Old Testament, questions about various translations, questions about the Greek Septuagint (LXX), questions about theology, questions about Calvinism, questions about Gail Riplinger, questions about women preachers, questions about the Bible's inspiration, and questions about twenty-two miscellaneous topics.

- **Various Questions and Answers Might Be Similar**. I have tried not to duplicate questions and answers in this fourth book. However, various things should be understood by the readers. Similar questions might have been asked in books one, two, three, or four. Similar questions might also have been asked in this fifth book. But if there is a slightly different emphasis either in the question, or in my answer, I have included them. Be sure to consult the very detailed INDEX in this book to help you.

D. A. Waite

Pastor D. A. Waite, Th.D., Ph.D.

Director of the **Bible For Today**, Incorporated, and

Pastor of the **Bible For Today Baptist Church**

Table of Contents

The Fifth 200 Questions Answered By Dr. D. A. Waite

?

Introductory Considerations

Have you received your copy of *THE FIRST 200 QUESTIONS ANSWERED* (**BFT #3909 @ $12.00 + $7.00 S&H**)? Have you received your copy of *THE SECOND 200 QUESTIONS ANSWERED* (**BFT #3473 @ $12.00 + $7.00 S&H**)? Have you received your copy of *THE THIRD 200 QUESTIONS ANSWERED* (**BFT #3482 @ $12.00 + $7.00 S&H**)? Have you received your copy of *THE FOURTH 200 QUESTIONS ANSWERED* (**BFT #3482 @ $12.00 + $7.00 S&H**)? If not, you might want to get a copy of each of these books and read them along with the present book of THE FOURTH 200 QUESTIONS ANSWERED (**BFT #3494 @ $15.00 + $7.00 S&H**).

Though there might be questions here that were included in either the first, second, third, or fourth book, they are asked by different people at different times and in different ways. My answers are also different in various ways. As in the first, second, third, and fourth question and answer books, I have included an extensive index of both words and phrases. You might have a specific topic that you are seeking answers to. Try to find it in the Index. I hope I have included it.

CHAPTER I
QUESTIONS ABOUT
THE KING JAMES BIBLE

The KJB And Faith's Foundation
QUESTION #801

1. Perhaps I didn't quite understand your statement ["*it is not the words of the English King James Bible that are the foundation of our Christian faith*"]:

a. Did you mean that they are not the foundation of our [English speakers'] Christian faith today, i.e., in this day and age?

b. If someone today doesn't know Greek, Hebrew, and Aramaic, does he or does he not have a completely trustworthy and firm foundation in the King James Bible for his Christian faith? (I refer here to English speakers.)

2. Again, perhaps I didn't quite understand what you were getting at, but the following questions came to mind based on what you wrote:

a. Are the words of the English King James Bible the completely trustworthy foundation of English speakers' Christian faith today?

b. Are there errors in the King James Bible somewhere which would negate or preclude it being the completely and 100% accurately preserved words of God in English without mistake?

c. Why aren't the "words of the English King James Bible" the completely secure foundation for our Christian faith today?

ANSWER #801

1. I stand by my words, "*it is not the words of the English King James Bible that are the foundation of our Christian faith.*"

a. The King James Bible is an excellent translation of that "FOUNDATION," but it is man's translation or interpretation of that "FOUNDATION" rather than God's own WORDS themselves. To make the King James Bible the "FOUNDATION," like Gail Riplinger and Peter Ruckman do, and to scuttle the Hebrew, Aramaic, and Greek genuine and REAL FOUNDATION, I believe is a sad and fast-growing theological heresy in our country and around the world.

b. If someone today doesn't know Greek, Hebrew, and Aramaic, does he or does he not have a completely trustworthy and firm foundation in the King James Bible for his Christian faith? (I refer here to English speakers.)

He has a "firm foundation" in a SECONDARY WAY, but must NEVER think this is the REAL AND GENUINE "FOUNDATION."

2. More questions:

a. Are the words of the English King James Bible the completely trustworthy foundation of English speakers' Christian faith today?

b. Are there errors in the King James Bible somewhere which would negate or preclude it being the completely and 100% accurately preserved words of God in English without mistake?

c. Why aren't the "words of the English King James Bible" the completely secure foundation for our Christian faith today?

There need not be any "errors" in translation of the King James Bible, or any translation, yet you must NEVER exalt ANY TRANSLATION (including the King James Bible) above God's own Words which He Himself has given to us and PRESERVED for us. That is the heresy I wish to oppose strongly against the Ruckman/Riplinger coalition and their followers. Perhaps you are one of their followers yourself. If so, I would strongly disagree with you on this point, though would agree with you on the accuracy, faithfulness, and excellent TRANSLATION of the King James Bible. The King James Bible is NOT "*inspired*," "*inspired of God*," "*given by inspiration of God*," "*verbally inspired*," or "*God-breathed*" as the HEBREW, ARAMAIC, AND GREEK WORDS that God Himself gave us. If you believe any of these five terms can be used for the King James Bible or any other translation, I must part company with you.

KJB Superior to the Geneva Bible
QUESTION #802

I do appreciate the NOTES from which you preached 2 Peter and the audio lessons from John. Both came through with no problems. I would like it if you could send me other NOTES as well. Regarding the NOTES on 2 Peter, did you take those pages into the pulpit and preach from them, or did you have a truncated version of them?

Please allow me to ask you a question regarding the Geneva Bible and the King James Bible. If both are based on the same Hebrew and Greek manuscripts, why is it that the King James Bible is considered superior? I have a copy of the 1599 version published Tolle Lege Press and I have noticed that different English words represent those of the original manuscripts.

ANSWER #802

I'm glad the NOTES and John came through all right. I'll be glad to send you the NOTES for 2 Peter 2 and 3 in this E-mail. After I mark up the NOTES, adding any other things by way of application, I take the notes into the pulpit, and use them by reading and commenting briefly on the other verses, and referring to the Greek meanings as needed on certain verbs, tenses, and nouns.

Though the Geneva Bible and the King James Bible were taken from the same Hebrew, Aramaic, and Greek Words, the King James Bible is more accurate than the Geneva Bible. John Reynolds, one of the leading King James Bible translators, asked King James to authorize a new translation. The reason that he gave to King James was: *"the versions extant,* [were] *not answering to the originals."* By the "versions extant" or then in existence, Reynolds included the Wycliffe, the Coverdale, the Great, the Geneva, the Bishops, the and other Bibles of his day. Though I have not compared the Geneva with the King James Bible verse by verse, I take John Reynolds at his word as the reason for having a new translation. The Geneva Bible also had many hyper-Calvinist notes which the King James Bible translators did not want to include.

The KJB'S Underlying Greek Text
QUESTION #803

In listening to your broadcasts on Bible texts, and in listening to Dr. Frank Logsdon, Mitch Cannup, and Pastor Jack Moorman, some questions arise that I would like answered.

What is the Greek Text that underlies the King James Bible? Is it the Erasmus text, the Daniel Bomberg text, the F. H. A Scrivener text, or the Beza text? I have heard this text connected to all of these and perhaps some more names.

Mitch Cannupp indicated that maybe F. H. A. Scrivener may have back-translated a text into Greek.

Is there a way to make this clear as to just what did take place, and how all of these people can be claimed to have such a great influence on the Greek that underlies the King James Bible? I guess I don't understand how all of these people could be an integral part of this text, given that these people did not live during the same times. Is there a book out there that explains where all of these people come in to play with the Greek?

ANSWER #803

The text underlying the New Testament of the King James Bible is Beza's 5th edition, 1598 as printed in Scrivener's Greek Text. The Masoretic Hebrew Daniel Bomberg edition is the Hebrew Text underlying the Old Testament of the King James Bible. Dr. Scrivener lists only 190 places in the New Testament where the King James Bible translators used some other Greek source than Beza's 5th edition. Since there are over 140,000 Greek Words in the Greek New Testament, 190 is only a tiny fraction of the entire New Testament.

It is a total lie that Dr. Scrivener "back-translated" from the King James Bible to Greek as Gail Riplinger and others like James Price have repeated over and over again. There is not one scintilla of proof of this false statement.

The KJB's Use By Dr. L. S. Chafer
QUESTION #804

In listening to the Systematic Theology class, I found myself becoming curious about Dr. Lewis Sperry Chafer's position on the King James Bible. In some of the class videos, it sounded like Dr. Chafer was "loose" in his use of the King James Bible.

ANSWER #804

Dr. Lewis Sperry Chafer used the King James Bible mostly in his Theology Book, but his Seminary that I attended (Dallas Theological Seminary) from 1948 through 1953 used the Gnostic Critical Greek text in all of their Greek classes. The teachers recommended the American Standard Version of 1901 which was based upon this false Gnostic Critical Greek text. Chafer was adversely influenced by the Gnostic Critical Westcott and Hort Greek Text that came out in 1881. Chafer's theology in other areas is conservative. After Dr. Chafer's death in 1952, Dr. Walvoord, the next president of the school, changed Dr. Chafer's Scripture verses to the New International Version (NIV).

The Defense of the KJB
QUESTION #805

My husband is a Pastor. I am looking for teaching materials regarding not only the history of, but the "*defense*" of, the King James Bible. I own a *Defined King James Bible* and love it. The town we live in is very "churched" and I really want to give these young people some "meat" to help them learn more about the Lord's Word.

ANSWER #805

I suggest you get my book, *DEFENDING THE KING JAMES BIBLE* (**BFT #1594**) It is $12 + $8.00 S&H. In the Appendix, there are over 1,000 other titles that defend the King James Bible. In the book, I present four superiorities of the King James Bible: (1) Texts, (2) Translators, (3) Translation Technique, and (4) Theology. You can call **856-854-4452** and order with your credit card if that is easier.

The KJB's Marginal Notes
QUESTION #806
What was involved in the marginal notes in the original King James Bible of 1611? Do they always indicate textual variants?

ANSWER #806

The marginal notes in the King James Bible of 1611 only rarely indicated textual "*variants.*" Most of their notes were alternate possible translations, not alternate texts. The King James translators believed they had the right Hebrew, Aramaic, and Greek Words from which to translate. The new translation people have often tried to imply that all of the marginal notes indicated textual variants. This is false.

KJB Not a Replacement
QUESTION #807
Does the King James Bible replace the original Hebrew, Aramaic, and Greek? Was the King James Bible "*inspired*"?

ANSWER #807
The King James Bible is the only faithful, true, and accurate English translation in existence, but it was not "*given by inspiration of God,*" "*inspired of God,*" "*verbally inspired,*" "*God-breathed*" or "*inspired* in any sense whatever.*" To use any of these five terms about the King James Bible, or about any translation, makes you a follower of both Peter Ruckman, and Gail Riplinger, and others who are heretics on the "*inspiration*" of the King James Bible and on many other things. I suggest you remove these words when talking about our King James Bible. All of these terms rightly belong only to the Hebrew, Aramaic, and Greek Words that God Himself spoke, and not to those Words translated by men into the languages of the world. The King James Bible does not replace the Hebrew, Aramaic, and Greek Words as Gail Riplinger and Peter Ruckman erroneously teach. If you want to discuss this further, you can call me at **856-854-4747** and we can talk about it.

Terms Used To Describe the KJB?
QUESTION #808
Is the King James Bible an error-free translation in which each word is God speaking, or does it contain errors as do all the other translations? It either is or isn't God's inerrant Word.

ANSWER #808

I do not say there are *"translation errors"* in the King James Bible. However, I don't like to use certain terms and words which I reserve for God and His Hebrew, Aramaic, and Greek Words that He actually gave to us. Those words, and those alone can exclusively be called *"inspired, inerrant, infallible, perfect, pure, and preserved."* These words cannot properly be used of the King James Bible, or any other translation made by man.

The King James Bible translators used very poor judgment in their 1611 inclusion of the Apocrypha which is filled with errors and apostasy. You cannot distance the 1611 King James Bible from the Apocrypha and its errors.

The Word Spelling In the KJB

QUESTION #809

Why do some King James Bibles have the word *"throughly"* and some use the word *"thoroughly"* in 2 Timothy 3:17 for example?

It seems to me the 1611 King James Bible has the spelling that can be confusing as well. For example, the "S" looks different. Is this correct?

ANSWER #809

The Cambridge King James Bible (which is what our *Defined King James Bible* is) has the proper spelling in 2 Timothy 3:17. It is *"throughly."* Many of the other American-made King James Bible's spell the word, *"thoroughly."* This is an error. It is a departure from the proper spelling as found in the original King James Bible of 1611 and its official revisions.

You are correct that the "S" in the original 1611 looks something like an "f" rather than an "S." The original spellings are different as well, such as spelling *"sin"* as *"sinne."* Other spelling examples are: *"Heaven"* is *"heauen"* (Genesis 1:1); *"form"* is *"forme"* (Genesis 1:2); *"void"* is *"voyd"* (Genesis 1:2); *"upon"* is *"vpon"* (Genesis 1:2); *"deep"* is *"deepe"* (Genesis 1:2); and *"moved"* is *"mooued."* There are hundreds and even thousands of similar spelling changes, though such changes do not affect the meaning of the word in question.

Cambridge & Oxford KJB Editions

QUESTION #810

I know that the 1769 edition had two versions, the Cambridge and the Oxford. Which one is commonly called the King James Bible in popular use? Also, aren't there some minor differences in wording between the two?

ANSWER #810

There are many "editions" of the King James Bible published by publishers in the USA such as Kregel, Eerdmans, Moody, Zondervan, etc.

Only two are official from Britain, the Cambridge and the Oxford. These are under "*cum privilegio*" ("*with privilege*" or copyright). Of these two, the Cambridge is far more accurate than the Oxford. Our *Defined King James Bible* has used the Cambridge edition. The Old Scofield Reference Bible, for example, uses the Oxford edition. I have a list of some of the differences between these two editions. Though some might be minor, they are still differences.

KJB Spelling Differences
QUESTION #811

Luke 17:27 "*They did eat, they drank, they married wives, they were given in marriage, until the day that **Noe** entered into the ark, and the flood came, and destroyed them all.*"
In this verse from the King James Bible, there is a reference of "*Noe.*" Why isn't is "*Noah*"?

ANSWER #811

In this verse, "*Noe*" is used because it is the transliteration, letter for letter, of the Greek word, NOE. "*Noah*" in the Old Testament is the transliteration, letter for letter, of the word, NOACH. The King James Bible does the same for "*Esaias,*" "*Jeremy,*" "*Elias,*" and other transliteration words in the Greek New Testament rather than using the Hebrew transliterations. Some English translations, however, do not transliterate these names, but use the Old Testament Hebrew letters rather than the New Testament Greek letters.

KJB Translators' Opinions
QUESTION #812

Robert Joyner claims to use the writings of the King James Bible translators to "destroy" the claims of the King James Bible believers. Do you have some comments or references I can use in contending for the King James Bible online about this view? There are the usual lies and exaggerations in these claims, but what seems to impress my opponents is that Joyner claims to use the words of the translators themselves against our view of the supremacy of the King James Bible today. I doubt very much they have actually read the King James Bible's *Epistle Dedicatory* for themselves and reasoned from it to this conclusion. And sadly they don't seem to be interested in any information that disagrees with what they already believe. But I would like to reply reasonably to this point about the translators' opinions supposedly refuting the superiority claims of those who defend the King James Bible today.

ANSWER #812

I do not believe we should use the words of the King James Bible translators in their *Epistle Dedicatory*, their *Preface*, or anywhere else. They were members of the Church of England. I differ with many of their doctrinal beliefs being a Bible-believing Baptist. It is their translation of the King James Bible that we should defend as accurate, not necessarily their opinions about other matters.

I have found that these Gnostic Critical Text brethren will not be changed, nor are they interested in any information to make them change. It is like trying to walk into a stone wall. Robert Sumner and Robert Joyner, and their kin, are the stone wall. They use false statements, distortions, and "straw men" to convince their readers. I believe it is a waste of time to answer them or dignify their answers. I believe the proper position and answer is to send out the true position to all who will listen. *Defending the King James Bible* and many other books and booklets can be used to do this as found on our Bible For Today (BibleForToday.org) and Dean Burgon Society (DeanBurgonSociety.org) websites.

The KJB and Bible Maps

QUESTION #813

I recently purchased a *Defined King James Bible* from a store in Texas through the internet. I found that the maps at the back were incorrect in there placement of the land of "*Palestine*" in the time of Jesus. This is surely not right in the light of known history that the word, "*Palestine*," was only in existence after the emperor Hadrian renamed Israel, Palestine after the Jewish revolt in 135 A.D. Can you clear this up for me as this is only but one of the incorrect claims. Is the *Defined King James Bible* I have a bogus one? I spent a lot of time trying to find a proper Bible with correct translation and this was recommended to me as one of the best. I am somewhat disappointed now.

ANSWER #813

The maps you have in that Bible were taken from another publisher and used with permission. They are the same in all of our *Defined King James Bibles*. Unless I missed it, the word, "*Palestine*," only appears on map #6. It says "*Palestine or Israel*." The caption at the top of the map is "*MAJOR NATIONS OF THE BIBLE THEN AND NOW*." "*Palestine*" is the "*NOW*." "*Israel*" is the "*THEN*." That map is not "*incorrect*" as you have charged. It is correct. If you are interested in the finest, most accurate, and correct English translation of the Bible, our *Defined King James Bible* which you have in your possession is the one to have and to use. As you know, maps are not part of the translation of the Bible, however upset you might be by them.

The Defense of the KJB

QUESTION #814

Is your printed book on *Defending the King James Bible* considered a more thorough work than the video seminars, or will they each contain information that is possibly different yet complimentary to one another?

Can you point out a resource that you offer that might be helpful for the layperson like myself to explain these issues to others, preferably without having their eyes glazing over? I have shared much of what I have learned with friends, family members, co-workers and even my previous employer in as much of a non-confrontational way as is possible, but with few exceptions they do not see the problem with new translations.

ANSWER #814

The King James Bible Seminar gives much more material than I have in my book, *Defending the King James Bible.* I have over 500 Power Point slides as I explain the details of the superiority of the Greek Text underlying the King James Bible and the superiority of the King James Bible itself. Both sources are helpful and contain materials that complement each other. I would recommend that you begin with my book first. It explains the superiority of the King James Bible, over any other English translation, in four important areas: (1) superior texts; (2) superior translators; (3) superior translation technique; and superior theology.

So-Called "Errors" in the KJB

QUESTION #815

I believe, as you also appear to do, that the correct version of the King James Bible is the Word of God in English for today. But, what am I to do when confronted with the following alleged "*errors*" in the King James Bible? I note that these alleged "*errors*" came from the heretic, Herbert W. Armstrong.

ANSWER #815

I believe you should do nothing when confronted by these "*alleged*" and very few so-called "*errors*" in the King James Bible. From the few I checked on that you gave me, they are not "*translation errors.*" Aside from this, there appears to be no willingness to be alarmed about the real errors that I have documented in my research writing. There are 2,000 real errors in the New King James Version. There are over 4,000 real errors in the New American Standard Version. There are many more than 6,653 real errors in the New International Version. In other words, their focus is incorrect. It should have been on and against the false error-laden modern versions. It is they that should be trashed, rather than the King James Bible.

CHAPTER II
QUESTIONS ABOUT
THE NEW TESTAMENT

Replacement of the Apostle Judas
QUESTION #816

My daughter and I were studying this morning about the selection in Acts Chapter 1 of Matthias as the apostle to replace. The decision was committed to God, in prayer. They used the Old Testament method of selecting a scapegoat. The selection of Matthias does not exclude Paul since the number of apostles seems larger than the 12. Barnabas is called an apostle in Acts 14:14, James in Galatians 1:19, and Apollos in I Corinthians 4:6-9.

ANSWER #816

While it is true that other men were called "apostles" in the New Testament, the question that many raise is (if God really wanted to replace Judas as an apostle) who was the "apostle" that God replaced him with? Was it Matthias, or was it Paul? My personal opinion is that it was Paul for several reasons.

1. The apostles ordered by the Lord Jesus Christ to "*tarry*" until they were "*endued with power from on high.*" Instead, the apostles held an election with only two nominees. [**Luke 24:49** "*And, behold, I send the promise of my Father upon you: but **tarry** ye in the city of Jerusalem, until ye be **endued with power** from on high.*"]

2. Every one of the twelve apostles was selected by the Lord Jesus Christ Himself. (Matthew 10:1-4; Luke 6:13). Mathias was not selected by the Lord Jesus Christ, but by the apostles. Paul was selected by the Lord Jesus Christ.

Meanings Of N.T. Words
QUESTION #817

Concerning Romans 16:7, I have 3 questions:

1. Is the second person, Junia, a man or a woman?

2. Andronicus and Junia are said to be kinsmen; other translations give "*relatives*," or "*Jews*." Is it a family kind of relative of each other, or is it a family as "Jews" as being relatives of Paul?

3. Can you give me an explanation as to why Andronicus and Junia are "*of note among the apostles*"? In the newer versions, it seems that they were apostles themselves.

ANSWER #817

1. Junia was a woman. She was one of Paul's "*kinsmen*" or "fellow countryman" and a "*fellow prisoner.*"

2. Andronicus was a man. He was also one of Paul's "*kinsmen*" or 'fellow countryman" and a "*fellow prisoner.*"

3. The Greek word, APOSTOLOS, also has a wider meaning of "*other eminent Christian teachers.*"

What Does "Q" Stand For?

QUESTION #818

What is "Q"? Is it a good doctrine to study and follow?

ANSWER #818

As I understand it, "Q" stands for the German word, "Quellen." It is said to be a source for some of the Gospels such as Mark. It is a false higher critical made-up source that cannot be proven even to exist. It should not be followed under any circumstances.

The "Feast of the Dedication"

QUESTION #819

I heard Dr. Mal Couch say that, "*I guess Christ was wrong to go up to Jerusalem to Hanukkah, the festival of Lights*" (John 10:22). Did Jesus really celebrated this feast?

ANSWER #819

The Lord Jesus Christ was not "*wrong*" in anything He did. It is not right to accuse Him of being "*wrong.*" Furthermore, there is no Biblical proof that this "*feast*" was Hanukkah. The "*feast*" is not called Hanukkah. It is just called "*the feast of the dedication.*" It is not called "*the festival of Lights.*"

Church Fathers For 1 John 5:7-8

QUESTION #820

I listened to your sermon defending on 1 John5:7-8. Please tell me the names of those church fathers that have mentioned these verses.

ANSWER #820

Here are a few church fathers and other evidences given by Dr. Jack Moorman in his excellent article on 1 John 5:7-8 (**BFT #1617**).

"The following gives some of the testimony for the disputed words in the Latin West before 550":

1. A passage in the writings of Tertullian (died 220) has often been cited as indicating that this Father knew of the words. Many deny this, and say that Tertullian's statement is to be limited to John 16:14 and 10:30.

> He saith, *"He shall take of mine,"* even as He Himself of the Father. Thus the connexion of the Father in the Son, and of the Son in Paraclete, maketh Three that cohere together one from the other: which Three are one Substance, not one Person; as it is said, *"I and My Father are one,"* in respect to unity of essence, not to singularity of number (adv. Praxean, c. 25).

2. Cyprian of Carthage (died 258) refers very plainly to the disputed words:

> The Lord saith, *"I and the Father are one;"* and again it is written concerning the Father, Son and Holy Spirit, *"And three are one"* (de Catholicae ecclesiae unitate, c. 6).

Critics have argued that Cyprian was merely giving a Trinitarian interpretation to verse 8.

> The spirit, and the water, and the blood: and these three agree in one. The answer to this is plain; the figures of verse 8 cannot <u>naturally</u> be interpreted as the <u>Persons</u> of the Holy Trinity.

It is further argued that Facundus (c.550) a bishop of Cyprian's church interpreted verse 8 as referring to the Trinity and quotes Cyprian's statement as supporting his view. This is countered by pointing out that Fulgentius of the same church who wrote a little earlier quotes Cyprian as referring to verse seven.

3. Priscillian, a Spanish Christian executed on a charge of heresy in AD 385, clearly quotes the words in his "Liber Apologeticus."

Two other works quoting the passage may be as early if not earlier than Priscillian.

4. The "Speculum," a treatise which contains the Old Latin text, has the words. This work was written not later than the first half of the fifth century. However, the manner in which the passage is worded points to a date earlier than Priscillian (e.g. certainly for the passage, if not the Speculum itself).

5. A creed known as *"Expositio Fidei"* quotes the passage. Of this work the International Critical Commentary in 1 John says:

> *"The evidence of the "Expositio Fidei" published by Caspari from the Ambrosian MS... is also important. The close agreement of this with Priscillian's quotation is evident... Caspari, its editor, regards*

the creed as African, of the fifth or sixth century. Dom Morin would attribute it to Isaac the Jew and the times of Damasus (372). Kunstle regards it as clearly anti-Priscillianist..." (pp 158,59).

6. The passage is found in **r** , an Old Latin MS of the 5th or 6th century.

7. The words are quoted in a confession of faith drawn up by Eugenius, Bishop of Cartage in 484. This was presented by the bishops (note the plural!) of North Africa to vandal King Hunnerich. The Confession is found in "Historia Persecutionis," a 7th century work.

8. Two works either by, or associated with, Vigilus of Thapsus, in North Africa, (490) give the passage. These are vol. 1 of "de Trinitate," and "Contra Varimadum."

9. Fulgentius of Ruspe in North Africa (died 533) quotes the passage in "De fide Catholica adv. Pintam."

10. Though the early Vulgate MS (Fuldensis, 546) does not have the disputed words, it is quoted in the manuscript's prologue to the General Epistles.

11. Casslodorus (480-570) of Italy quotes the passage.

"Therefore, early testimony for this key Trinitarian verse does exist. It must be borne in mind that the above do not merely formulate the words for a treatise or creed, but quote them as an actual part of the text of 1 John."

What Is a "Deaconess"?

QUESTION #821

How would you interpret Romans 16:1 whom Paul calls Phoebe a *"deaconess"*? Are woman allowed to be elected as a *"deaconess"*? If not, how would you interpret Romans 16:1?

ANSWER #821

You are not correct that Phoebe was called a *"deaconess."*

*"I commend unto you Phoebe our sister, which is a **servant** of the church which is at Cenchrea:"* (Romans 16:1)

The Greek word used here is DIAKONON. Though it is sometimes transliterated as *"deacon,"* the word itself merely means:

"servant, one who serves, without necessarily having the office of deacon (Mt 20:26; Ro 16:1; Eph 6:21; 1Th 3:2)."

This is the meaning in Romans 16:1 when referring to Phoebe. I believe it is unscriptural to have women *"deacons"* fulfilling the office of a *"deacon"* in a local church. I say this because 1 Timothy 3:12 says very clearly, *"Let the deacons be the **husbands of one wife**."* This makes it clear that those in the office as *"deacons"* in a local church must be males, not females.

The Year of Christ's Birth
QUESTION #822
I was reading a part of the book, *In the Fullness Of Time*, by Dr. Paul L. Maier. He said that Herod the Great died in 4 B.C. He believes the Lord Jesus Christ was born between 5 and 4 B.C. It it true that Jesus was born between 5 and 4 B. C.? I always thought Jesus was born in 1 A. D. Which is the truth?

ANSWER #822
Because of the various calendars that were used, the date is not too clear. http://customsholidays.suite101.com/article.cfm/the_year_of_jesus__birth indicates His birth at around 4 B.C. The following site agrees with 4 B.C. http://www.cgg.org/index.cfm/fuseaction/Library.sr/CT/ARTB/k/568/When-Was-Jesus-Born.htm. The link below puts the date at between 6 and 4 B.C. http://en.wikipedia.org/wiki/Nativity_of_Jesus#Date_of_birth

The Meaning Of Matthew 11:21
QUESTION #823
I'm having trouble understanding something in Matthew 11:21. The Bible tells us that if the cities of Tyre and Sidon had seen the mighty works of the Lord Jesus Christ that were done in Chorazin and Bethsaida, they would have come to repentance. But they didn't get to see them. That sounds like there are going to be those that would have been saved if some other plan had been used to do it. Or if they had been born at another time and lived in another place, they would have been saved (come to repentance). Could you help clarify this for me?

ANSWER #823
I think this is merely teaching that there were more miracles of the Lord Jesus Christ done in Chorazin and Bethsaida than in Tyre and Sidon. They had much light. If the same number of miracles were done in Tyre and Sidon, they would have repented and come to Christ. They had less light than the others. A similar contrast is mentioned in Matthew 11:23 and 24 which compares the miracles the Lord Jesus Christ performed in Capernaum with those that might have been done in Sodom. Though Capernaum did not repent, Sodom would have repented.

Holy "Ghost" Or Holy "Spirit"
QUESTION #824

Why did the King James Bible translators use the word "*Spirit*" in some places and then "*Ghost*" in others when referring to the third person of the Trinity?

ANSWER #824

We really don't know why "*Ghost*" and "*Spirit*" are both used in the King James Bible. Some say "*Ghost*" is when the relation to the Trinity is emphasized. We really don't know definitively. In 1611, "*Ghost*" meant "*Spirit*," though today it has quite a different meaning. In the King James Bible, "*Holy Spirit*" is used only seven times, two times in the Old Testament, and five times in the New Testament. "*Holy Ghost*" is used 90 times in 89 verses. Perhaps, the real reason should be why did the King James Bible translators not use "*Holy Ghost*" in all 97 references since "*Ghost*" meant "*Spirit*" in 1611.

"Taken" Or "Wanting"?
QUESTION #825

"*Two men shall be in the field; the one shall be <u>taken</u>, and the other left.*" (Luke 17:36)

Can you explain Luke 17:36 and the use of "*taken*" rather than "*wanting*" in the verse. It seemed to be the only example Mark Minnick could really come up with in regards to pointing out something he thought was a problem in the King James Bible. I'm not sure what "*wanting*" would mean in that verse or why they think that could be the word there.

ANSWER #825

"<u>Taken</u>" is in the verse and the entire verse is present in our Textus Receptus Greek Text. What Mark Minnick means by "*wanting*" probably is that the entire verse 17:36 is "*wanting*," (not there) in the Gnostic Critical Text that he uses and defends. For the manuscript evidence in support of this verse, you can consult page 187 of Dr. Jack Moorman's book, *Early Manuscripts, Church Fathers, and the Authorized Version* (**BFT #3230 @ $20.00 + $7.00 S&H**).

Meaning of "Taken" in Luke 17:36

QUESTION #826

In Luke 17:36, how do you understand "*taken*"? Where are these people "*taken*"?

ANSWER #826

Though some have interpreted this verse to mean these people were "*taken*" in the rapture, I believe the context tells quite a different story.

"*And they answered and said unto him, **Where**, Lord? And he said unto them, **Wheresoever the body is, thither will the eagles be gathered together**.*" (Luke 17:37)

It appears clearly that these people will be "*taken*" in judgment. Their bodies will be consumed by the flesh-eating birds of prey called here as the "*eagles*."

Bible Greek and Modern Greek

QUESTION #827

What language did the Lord Jesus Christ speak while on earth, Hebrew or Greek? Is the Bible Greek language the same as the modern Greek?

ANSWER #827

The Lord, no doubt, spoke Aramaic (a form of Hebrew) but he also spoke Greek which was current in His day. The Romans would not have understood Aramaic. Bible Greek is different from modern Greek in many ways though some of it is the same. Pronunciation, spelling, some word meanings, and rules for grammar are different. The Greek letters are the same, however.

Meaning Of Hebrews 6:4-9

QUESTION #828

I was reading Hebrews 6:4-9. Could you explain it to me please?

ANSWER #828

Hebrews 6:4 For it is impossible for those who were once enlightened, and have tasted of the heavenly gift, and were made partakers of the Holy Ghost, Hebrews 6:5 And have tasted the good word of God, and the powers of the world to come, Hebrews 6:6 If they shall fall away, to renew them again unto repentance; seeing they crucify to themselves the Son of God afresh, and put him to an open shame. Hebrews 6:7 For the earth which drinketh in the rain that cometh oft upon it, and bringeth forth herbs meet for them by whom it is dressed, receiveth blessing from God: Hebrews 6:8 But that which beareth thorns and briers is rejected, and is nigh unto cursing; whose end is to be burned. Hebrews 6:9 But, beloved, we are persuaded better things of you, and things that accompany salvation, though we thus speak.

I believe Paul was writing to "*holy brethren, partakers of the heavenly blessing.*" (Hebrews 3:1). <u>They were genuine Christians</u>. They were specially enlightened with much light and truth that was showered upon them. If they "*fall away*" from fellowship with the Lord (not losing their salvation) with all the light that God has given them, they will reach the place in their life that they will no longer repent. It becomes impossible for them to repent. They have chosen to live for the flesh the rest of their life. It may be that, because of their waywardness, they may commit the sin unto physical death and God will then take them Home to Heaven because of their disobedience (1 John 5:16). <u>I do not believe these people were lost people. Neither do I believe they were saved and then could lose their salvation.</u> As all genuine Christians, they could lose their fellowship with the Lord Jesus Christ, but never their salvation.

New Testament Colophons
QUESTION #829
Can you tell me where the "*colophons*" came from? When were they placed at the end of the books?
ANSWER #829
One website has defined a "*colophon*" as follows:
"*A brief description of publication or production notes relevant to the edition, in modern books usually located at the reverse of the title page, but can also sometimes be located at the end of the book.*"

<u>Where Bible "*colophons*" came from is not clear.</u> They probably were added by the copyist who copied the manuscript from the original writer. New Testament colophons are placed at the end of the book in question.

Searching the Scriptures In Berea
QUESTION #830
In Acts 17:11, of those living in Berea, it reads:
"*These were more noble than those in Thessalonica, in that they received the word with all readiness of mind, and **searched the scriptures daily**, whether those things were*

so."

Did those in Berea know Hebrew, or did they know only Greek? If only Greek, did they use the Septuagint (LXX) Old Testament to "search"?

ANSWER #830

I don't believe the Septuagint (LXX) was in existence until the 200's A.D. in the time of Origen, so they could not have used it. Those in Berea might have known both Hebrew and Greek. I'm sure the *"Scriptures"* they *"searched"* were the Hebrew Old Testament Scriptures. The word for *"Scriptures"* is GRAPHE. In all 51 references, GRAPHE always refers to the Hebrew or Greek original Words--never to translations of those Words like the Septuagint (LXX).

Meaning of "Gird up Your Loins"

QUESTION #831

What does the phrase *"gird up your loins"* mean?

ANSWER #831

In 1 Peter 1:13, *"Gird up"* means:
"328 anazonnumi {an-ad-zone'-noo-mee}
from 303 and 2224;; v
AV - gird up 1; 1
1) to gird up
2) metaph. be prepared
2a) a metaphor derived from the practice of the Orientals, who in order to be unimpeded in their movements were accustomed, when starting a journey or engaging in any work, to bind their long flowing garments closely around their bodies and fastened them with a leather belt."

I think this explanation is clear.

Greek or Hebrew New Testament?

QUESTION #832

Could you please help me with this Bible question as I know you have deep understandings of this matter. Was the whole of the New Testament originally in Greek? Did Peter also write in Greek, or did he write in Hebrew? Someone has said the New Testament couldn't be in Greek since Jesus spoke Hebrew. Your answer would be enable me to fill this person in on the matter.

ANSWER #832

The New Testament was originally written in Greek, not Hebrew or Aramaic as some teach today. Though a few of Jesus' words in the New Testament are recorded in Aramaic, Greek was the language used by God to write down all of the events of His life on earth. Peter also wrote in Greek as did all the writers in the New Testament, including Paul, John, Jude, James, Matthew, Mark, and Luke. For those who say the New Testament was originally written in Aramaic, where are the manuscripts to prove this? There are presently over 5,500 Greek Manuscripts that have been preserved to this day, proving, by this evidence, that Greek was the original New Testament language. On the contrary, there are very few Aramaic translations in existence today compared to the 5,500 Greek manuscripts. The LINK below gives the history of this argument which began in a Nestorian man.

http://en.wikipedia.org/wiki/Aramaic_New_Testament

CHAPTER III
QUESTIONS ABOUT
ORIGINAL BIBLE TEXTS

What Was In the Qumran Caves?
QUESTION #833
Were the scrolls that the shepherd boy found in the Qumran caves of the Textus Receptus kind or the Critical texts of Vatican (B) and Sinai (Aleph)?

ANSWER #833
For a comprehensive analysis of all eleven Qumran caves, you should look up http://www.bibleplaces.com/qumrancaves.htm. This LINK tells in detail which Old Testament books were found in the various caves. There were no New Testament books found there.

Meaning of "MSS" and "BSA"
QUESTION #834
I am reading the book on *Gnosticism*. On page three, I can't understand the the meaning of "MSS" and "BSA." What do these mean?

ANSWER #834
"MSS" means "manuscripts." "BSA" is defined on page 24 the book on *Gnosticism*. "B" stands for the Vatican manuscript. "S" stands for the Sinai manuscript. "A" stands for the Alexandrian manuscript.

The Byzantine or Majority Text
QUESTION #835
Is the Byzantine (or Majority) Text the same with Textus Receptus? Is the Byzantine (or Majority) Text reliable?

ANSWER #835
The Byzantine (or Majority) Text is not the same as the Textus Receptus. In fact, there are now three different Greek New Testament texts that are called the Byzantine (or Majority) Text: (1) There is the Hodges-Farstad Majority Text; (2) There is the Robinson-Pierpont Majority Text; and (3) There is the

Wilbur Pickering Majority Text that is being developed. Estimates are that these texts, which differ from one another, change the Textus Receptus in about 1500 to 1800 places. I do not believe that any of these Byzantine (or Majority) Texts are reliable. I favor the Traditional New Testament Greek Words underlying the King James Bible. These Greek Words are found in Beza's 5th edition of 1598 and in *Scrivener's Annotated Greek New Testament* (BFT #1670 @ $35.00 + $7.00 S&H).

Sun "Eclipsed" or "Darkened"?
QUESTION #836
In Luke 23:45, does the Critical Greek Text say that there was an "*eclipse*" of the sun rather than referring to a special miracle that happened during the crucifixion of Christ"

Luke 23:45 "*And the sun **was darkened**, and the veil of the temple was rent in the midst.*" (King James Bible)
ANSWER #836
No matter what the translations for this verse might say, their false Gnostic Critical Greek Text reads: EKLIPTONTOS ("*was eclipsed*"). This denies that a miracle of God was performed, but that it was just a natural phenomenon that took place. The proper Traditional Greek Text reads ESKOTISTHE ("*was darkened*"). This shows that it was a miracle of God rather than merely a natural "*eclipse*" of the sun.

Michael Sproul Refuted
QUESTION #837
I am interested in a book that you have. But I wanted to find out a little more about it from you before I decide to buy. It is *A Critical Answer to Michael Sproul's God's Word Preserved*. Who is Michael Sproul? Why the need to respond to a book that Michael Sproul wrote? And how current is this issue regarding his serious errors? Was his book written years ago or more recently?
ANSWER #837
Sproul's book is fairly recent. My answer to his book came out in 2008. He is the chairman of the board of the International Baptist College and pastor of the Tri-State Baptist Church. Both of these institutions are in Tempe, Arizona. He's a fundamentalist leader who champions the Gnostic Critical Greek Text and fights against the Received Text and the King James Bible. He is a leader in his college and his church who is training men to believe his way. His book contains many serious errors that should be answered. I have

answered 275 of these errors in my book. It can be ordered as **BFT #3308 @ $15.00 + $7.00 S&H**.

The Gnostic Critical Greek Text

QUESTION #838

Is the Gnostic Critical Greek Text also known as the Alexandrian Text? Does it include both the Sinaiticus and Vaticanus codices?

ANSWER #838

Yes, the Gnostic Critical Greek Text is also know as the Alexandrian text. It is based on the Vatican and Sinai manuscripts.

The Sinai Manuscript

QUESTION #839

Does the Sinai codex contains parts of the Old Testament? Or only the New Testament?

ANSWER #839

http://www.codex-sinaiticus.net/en/codex/content.aspx   gives   you information on the books included in the Sinai manuscript. According to this article, it includes all of the New Testament and about half of the Old Testament.

Approximate Date of The Sinai MS

QUESTION #840

Codex Sinaiticus was written in the 4th century A.D. Is this correct? The Greek Orthodox Church says that Codex Sinaiticus is the oldest manuscript.

ANSWER #840

The 4th century date is the suggested date of the Sinai manuscript as well as the Vatican manuscript.   That does not mean either are the oldest manuscripts. The original New Testament manuscripts were from the first century. Fragments of the New Testament are much earlier than the 4th century, though they are not as complete as either the Vatican or the Sinai manuscripts.

Bishop Westcott's Heresies

QUESTION #841

Just recently, I was talking with a retired minister that attends the church where I have been going. I brought up the Bible text situation. He has stayed with the King James Bible. He is not so sure about the controversy about

Westcott and Hort, though. He said he has a book on the Gospel of John that Westcott wrote. He said that was one of the best he has ever read. Could you explain the seeming dichotomy about the other books that Westcott and Hort wrote which are obviously heretical, and then this Gospel of John which this retired minister believes is so excellent?

ANSWER #841

Westcott's book on the Gospel of John I have and have read. He speaks out of both sides of his pen in this book as well as his books on Hebrews and the Epistles of John. He seems to be conservative in some of the statements he makes, yet within all of his books there are many heresies that apparently this pastor did not find. In my book, *THE THEOLOGICAL HERESIES OF WESTCOTT AND HORT* (**BFT #595 @ $8.00 + $3.00 S&H**), I have listed around 125 quotations from Westcott's three books that represent latent heresies. In one my other books, *WESTCOTT'S CLEVER DENIAL OF THE BODILY RESURRECTION OF CHRIST* (**BFT #1131 @ $5.00 + $3.00 S&H**), you can see that Westcott has denied the bodily resurrection of the Lord Jesus Christ by his omission of it throughout his book on the resurrection.

The Traditional Received Text

QUESTION #842

What is the "Traditional" or "Received" Text? I do know what I believe and it is not the doctrine of Ruckman, Riplinger or Gipp, but I do need guidance from you.

ANSWER 842

I believe the "Traditional Text" or "Received Text" should be explained in a definite manner so that all will know what is meant. Since our Gnostic Critical Text brethren have laughed at us, saying that there are 10 or 15 so-called "Traditional Greek Texts," I have pinned down my definition very specifically. I define the Traditional Hebrew Text as being the exact Hebrew and Aramaic Words underlying the King James Bible. They are mostly those of the Jacob Ben Chayyim edition which is the Daniel Bomberg edition of 1525. I define the Traditional Greek Text as being the exact Greek Words underlying the King James Bible. They are mostly those of Beza's 5th Edition, 1598, as printed up by Dr. Frederick Scrivener's Greek Text.

In this way, nobody can say that I am unclear as to what I mean by these terms. This is a position based both on fact and on faith, but it is clear what I mean. It cuts through all of the Hebrew variations and all the Greek variations. I believe these Words underlying the King James Bible can be called "*Traditional*" and "*Received*" because they have been handed down through the centuries ("*Traditional*") and have also been received by Christians also down through the centuries ("*Received*")

On page 61 of my *DEFENDING THE KING JAMES BIBLE* book, I wrote:

> "*Basically, I would like to say that the New Testament foundation or basis for our Greek New Testament which underlies our KING JAMES BIBLE was definitely authorized and accepted by the churches down through the centuries, attested by the evidence, and therefore absolutely worthy of being trusted and believed by us today or in any future age!*"

I would say the same for the Old Testament:

> "*The Old Testament foundation or basis for our Hebrew Old Testament which unerlies our KING JAMES BIBLE was definitely authorized and accdepted by the churches down through the centuries, attested by the evidence, and therefore absolutely worthy of beng trust and believed ty us today or in any future age.*"

The Scofield Bible's Greek Text

QUESTION #843

C. I. Scofield was asked: "Which are the best manuscripts extant?" He replied "*Of the New Testament, the Sinaitic and Vatican.*" He also wrote:

> "*The discovery of the Sinaitic MS and the labours in the field of textual criticism of such scholars as Griesbach, Lachmann, Tischendorf, Tregelles, Winer, Alford and Westcott and Hort, have cleared the Greek "textus receptus" of minor inaccuracies, while confirming to a remarkable degree the general accuracy of the Authorized Version of that text.*"

In view of Scofield's view in favor of the Gnostic Critical Greek Text, should we recommend the Scofield Reference Bible?

ANSWER #843

It is clear that C. I. Scofield and his editors were sold out to the Gnostic Critical Greek Text of Westcott and Hort. Though the theology and notes are generally helpful, people should be warned not to believe any of their notes where they suggest words in the King James Bible should be changed. Other than that warning and a few other false views (such as the GAP theory) in that reference Bible, it is an overall help in Bible study.

New Testament Written in Greek
QUESTION #844

Some lady told me that the Book of Matthew was written in Hebrew. I looked for it through Google and found many lists on the Gospel of Matthew. I read some details on it. My questions about this is: Is it true that the Book of Matthew was written in Hebrew? Or is this a falsehood? I would appreciate that you give a short detail about it.

ANSWER #844

There are people who have said that, not only Matthew, but the entire New Testament was written in Aramaic (or Hebrew). I believe this is a falsehood. If this had been the original language, there would be over 5,500 Aramaic manuscripts of the N.T. in Aramaic (or Hebrew), but there are very, very few manuscripts in this "translation" of the Greek original. But there are over 5,500 manuscripts in the original New Testament Greek language. http://orvillejenkins.com/theology/primacyandpossiblity.html is an article that might help you on some of this.

NT Greek, Not Latin
QUESTION #845

When we talk about original Biblical languages, can we include Latin for the New Testament? Were there any Latin documents collated in the corpus of the Recieved Text?

ANSWER #845

We must limit "*original Biblical languages*" to just three, Hebrew, a very little Aramaic, and Greek. Latin should never be considered as an "*original Biblical Language*." Some are now saying that the New Testament was originally written in Latin. That is totally false. This falsehood possibly comes from the Roman Catholic Church that has, in the past, exalted Latin above all other languages. I don't know the source, but I know it to be false.

I'm sure Latin documents were "*collated*" but they are all copies made from one of the languages above. They should never be considered as originals.

On page 648 of *SCRIVENER'S ANNOTATED GREEK NEW TESTAMENT*, among the 190 quotes he lists for the King James Bible, other than Beza's 5th edition of 1598, the Latin Vulgate is listed for documents the King James Bible translators consulted, along with 9 other documents. 190 is a minute percentage of over 140,500 Greek Words in the New Testament of

Beza's 5th edition which was over 99% of cases the source for the King James Bible New Testament.

The Writing Over the Cross
QUESTION #846

Since the Gospels mention that on the cross Pilate wrote his inscription in Hebrew, Greek, and Latin, I was wondering if there exists any witness who wrote anything else besides that in Latin. I guess you already answered that.

ANSWER #846

Since these were the three major languages of the day in Palestine, (Hebrew, Greek, and Latin), Pilate put the statement in all of these languages on the cross so that everyone could read it in his own language. Luke 23:38 and John 19:20 have the only mention of "Latin" in the N.T. In Luke 23:38, the Gnostic Critical Text of the NASV, NIV, ESV and all the other modern verses based upon this false Greek Text omit all three of these languages, including Latin.

Catholic Priest and NA Greek Text
QUESTION #847

I was discussing with some pastors about the Critical Greek text of Nestle and Aland. I mentioned about the Jesuit priest being on the Nestle/Aland Committee and asked why would they do that? They (the pastor here and the one from Mark Minnick's ministry) mentioned that perhaps they had him because he was a textual expert of some sort. They did not seem to have any idea at all that a Jesuit Priest was on the Committee. Can you tell me how you found out about the Jesuit Priest being on the Nestle Aland Committee and any other information about this topic?

ANSWER #847

The current Nestle/Aland Committee with Father Carlo Martini on it is available. I got it from them:

http://en.wikipedia.org/wiki/Novum_Testamentum_Graece

It is a link on the Nestle/Aland Greek New Testament. It has the name of Father Carlo Martini on that committee.

http://en.wikipedia.org/wiki/Carlo_Maria_Martini is a link that gives the background of Martini's Jesuit career and death in August of 2012.

QUESTION #848

I very much appreciate your stand and that of the Dean Burgon Society. If you have time I would like to ask for some help. A Brother of mine is in his second year of seminary and is vacillating between the King James Bible and its underlying texts and the Critical Text position. He is taking New Testament Textual Criticism. One of his assignments is to translate and evaluate textual evidences. On the Syllabus, he is given a list of typical verses that are used such as Mark 1:1, the shorter ending of Mark, 1 John 5:7-8, the woman taken in adultery, etc. He knows where I stand and has asked my advice on 2 or 3 of the most important New Testament textual issues that are the harder ones to deal with. Could you give me some advice on how to advise him please or what you see as the most important N.T. textual issues.

ANSWER #848

First, is your brother willing to search for truth, or is he unwilling. All of these problem passages are due to the Gnostic Critical Greek text's false readings. If he is willing to see truth, I would recommend that he purchase and read *The Last Twelve Verses of Mark* by Dean John Burgon (**BFT #1139 @ $15.00 + $7.00 S&H**). I would also suggest that he also get a more recent book by Dr. Jack Moorman called *Early Manuscipts, Church Father, and the King James Bible* (**BFT #3230 @ $20.00 + $7.00 S&H**). If your brother is not interested in looking at the other side of the Gnostic Critical Greek Text, don't waste your time arguing with him. It will do no good.

CHAPTER IV
QUESTIONS ABOUT THE
CHINESE UNION VERSION

"Easter" vs. "Passover"
QUESTION #849

(1) Act 12:4 *"And when he had apprehended him, he put him in prison, and delivered him to four quaternions of soldiers to keep him; intending after* **Easter** *to bring him forth to the people."*

The CUV (Chinese Union Version) translated *"Easter"* as *"Passover."* At the present time *"Easter"* is translated as *"Resurrection Feast"* (in modern Chinese). Which translation is preferable?

(2) Act 12:20 *"And Herod was highly displeased with them of Tyre and Sidon: but they came with one accord to him, and, having made Blastus the king's chamberlain their friend, desired peace; because **their country** was nourished by the king's country."*

The CUV translated *"their country"* as *"their place"* or *"their region."* Should *"country,"* in this verse, be translated as *"nation"* instead ?

ANSWER #849

(1) Acts 12:4 uses the Greek word, PASCHA, which is translated everywhere else as *"passover."* Since it was already (verse 3) *"the feast of unleavened bread,"* it was already the 15th day of the first month (Leviticus 23:6). The *"passover"* was celebrated on the 14th day of first month (Leviticus 23:5). Perhaps this led the King James Bible to use *"easter"* which was the pagan feast ot ISHTAR that occurred around the same time as *"passover."* Since that was the feast being referred to, *"easter"* would be acceptable.

(2) Acts 12:20 uses *"country"* in the King James Bible. In the New Testament, it is used 15 times in the King James Bible. In the New Testament, *"region"* is also used. It is used 5 times. It should not be translated as *"nation."*

In English, here are some of the meanings of *"country."* It's a good word as it is.

coun•try (kun¿trÈ) pl. ©tries
noun

1. an area of land; region [wooded country]
2. the whole land or territory of a nation or state
3. the people of a nation or state
4. the land of a person's birth or citizenship
5. land with farms and small towns; rural region, as distinguished from a city or town
6. short for country music
adjective
1. of, in, or from a rural district
2. characteristic of or like that of the country; rustic
3. [Now Dial.] of one's own country; native
Etymology
[ME contre derived from OFr contrée derived from VL *(regio) contrata, region lying opposite derived from L contra: see contra-]

> In Greek, here are some of the meanings of the word, CHORA {kho'-rah} from a derivative of the base of 5490 through the idea of empty expanse;; n f
>
> AV - country 15, region 5, land 3, field 2, ground 1, coast 1; 27
>
> 1) the space lying between two places or limits
>
> 2) a region or country i.e. a tract of land
>
>   2a) the (rural) region surrounding a city or village, the country
>
>   2b) the region with towns and villages which surround a metropolis
>
> 3) land which is ploughed or cultivated, ground

"Disposition of Angels"
QUESTION #850

I have a question on a verse in the Chinese Union Version (CUV).

The King James Bible reads in Act 7:53: "*Who have received the law by the **disposition** of angels, and have not kept it.*"

The Chinese Union Version (CUV), the word, "*disposition*" was translated to "*to pass on*," or "*to preach*." We're not sure that "*disposition*" should be translated in this way.

ANSWER #850

The Greek word for "disposition" is DIATAGE. The meanings are as follows:

1296 diatage {dee-at-ag-ay'}
from 1299; TDNT - 8:36,1156; n f
AV - disposition 1, ordinance 1; 2
1) a disposition, arrangement, ordinance

In view of the meaning of DIATAGE, I would suggest either *"disposition,"* or *"arrangement."* Neither *"to pass on"* nor *"to preach"* would be the meaning or sense of this Greek word. Those would be incorrect meanings.

"Increased in Number"

QUESTION #851

We have question about Act 16:5: *"And so were the churches established in the faith, and **increased in number** daily."*

The Chinese Union Version (CUV) translated *"increased in number"* as *"number of people increased."* Does <u>*"number"* in this verse refer to *"churches"* or to *"people"*</u>?

ANSWER #851

The word for *"increased"* is:

4052 perisseuo {per-is-syoo'-o}
from 4053; TDNT - 6:58,828; v
AV - abound 17, abundance 3, remain 3, exceed 2, increase 2,
    be left 1, redound 1, misc 10; 39
1) **to exceed a fixed number** of measure, to be left over and
   above a certain number or measure
   1a) to be over, to remain
   1b) to exist or be at hand in abundance
      1b1) to be great (abundant)
      1b2) a thing which comes in abundance, or overflows unto one,
          something falls to the lot of one in large measure
      1b3) to redound unto, turn out abundantly for, a thing
   1c) to abound, overflow
      1c1) to be abundantly furnished with, to have in abundance,
          abound in (a thing), to be in affluence
      1c2) to be pre-eminent, to excel
      1c3) to excel more than, exceed
2) to make to abound
   2a) to furnish one richly so that he has abundance
   2b) to make abundant or excellent
"Abounding" is used of a flower going from a bud to full bloom.
   The word for *"number"* is:
706 arithmos {ar-ith-mos'}
from 142; TDNT - 1:461,78; n m
AV - number 18; 18
1) a fixed and definite number
2) an indefinite number, a multitude

ARITHMOS in turn, is from
142 airo {ah'-ee-ro}
a primary root; TDNT - 1:185,28; v
AV - take up 32, take away 25, take 25, away with 5, lift up 4,
     bear 3, misc 8; 102
1) to raise up, elevate, lift up
   1a) to raise from the ground, take up: stones
   1b) to raise upwards, elevate, lift up: the hand
   1c) to draw up: a fish
2) to take upon one's self and carry what has been raised up, to bear
3) to bear away what has been raised, carry off
   3a) to move from its place
   3b) to take off or away what is attached to anything
   3c) to remove
   3d) to carry off, carry away with one
   3e) to appropriate what is taken
   3f) to take away from another what is his or what is committed
      to him, to take by force
   3g) to take and apply to any use
   3h) to take from among the living, either by a natural death,
      or by violence
   3i) cause to cease

It does not mention "*number __of people__ increased*," but only "*increased in number*." This appears to refer back to the number of "*churches*" that "*increased in number daily*." In a translation, we should never go beyond what the Greek or Hebrew Words say by way of interpretation. We should never add words that are not there as they have done in the CUV.

"Way" or "Word"?
QUESTION #852

We have a question on Act 19:9. The Chinese Union Version (CUV) translated "*that way*" as "*this Word*." Should it be translated as "*way*," "*road*," or "*word*"?

> "*But when divers1 were hardened, and believed not, but spake evil of that __way__ before the multitude, he departed from them, and separated the disciples, disputing daily in the school of one Tyrannus.*" (Act 19:9)

ANSWER #852

As for *"way,"* *"road,"* or *"word,"* all the Greek texts read HODON or *"way"* or *"road."* None have *"word"* or anything like it. It is totally false to translate this word as *"word."*

"Venomous Beast"

QUESTION #853

I have a question on Acts 28:4:

> *"And when the barbarians saw the **venomous beast** hang on his hand, they said among themselves, No doubt this man is a murderer, whom, though he hath escaped the sea, yet vengeance suffereth not to live."*

The Chinese Union Version (CUV) translated *"venomous beast"* as *"viper."* We prefer to translate to *"venomous beast."* When I look at the Greek word, it said the word was THERION which meant a *"wild animal, or beast."*

ANSWER #853

Though the word, *"venomous"* is in italics, it is supplied for the meaning because this *"beast"* had poison which was supposed to kill Paul when it bit him (verses 5 and 6). THERION can mean, *"a wild animal, any living creature, not human, a beast."* Since this *"living creature"* did *"hang on his hand,"* it was probably a snake of some kind, whether a *"viper,"* an *"adder,"* a *"rattle snake,"* or some other brand of snake. I agree with you that you should keep either *"beast"* or *"snake"* which would be THERION, and include *"venomous"* because, from the context, it had poison in it.

"Things" or "Words"

QUESTION #854

I have a questions please help:

> Act 1:9 *"And when he had spoken these **things**, while they beheld, he was taken up; and a cloud received him out of their sight."*

In this verse, the Chinese Union Version (CUV) translated the word, *"**things**,"* to *"**words**"* (singular). We preferred to translate the word, *"**things**"* as in the King James Bible.

ANSWER #854

1. **In Acts 1:9**, the word for *"**things**"* is TAUTA. The meaning is as follows:

5023 **tauta** {tow'-tah}

nominative or accusative case neuter plural of 3778; pron

AV - these things 158, these 26, thus 17, that 7, these words 7, this 6, afterwards + 3326 4, misc 22; 247

1) these TAUTA is PLURAL hence "*things*" is accurate.

"All" and "Many"

QUESTION #855

Romans 5:18 *"Therefore as by the offence of one judgment came upon **all** men to condemnation; even so by the righteousness of one the free gift came upon **all** men unto justification of life."*

Romans 5:19 *"For as by one man's disobedience **many** were made sinners, so by the obedience of one shall **many** be made righteous."*

The Chinese Union Version (CUV) translated the word "*all*" and "*many*" in Romans 5:18-19 as the same word, "*folks*." Can "*many*" in verse 19 be translated as "*all*" as verse 18?

ANSWER #855

I don't think you can translate the POLLOI ("*many*") as "*all*." In v. 18, "*all*" is stated. Though in v. 19, "*many*" is the word used, yet in the context, it refers back to the "*all*" in verse 18. I think you should leave it the way the King James Bible has it which is an accurate translation of the Textus Receptus Greek Text.

CHAPTER V
QUESTIONS ABOUT THE
GREEK NEW TESTAMENT

Meaning of REMA
QUESTION #856
I hear charismatics use the word "REMA." What does this word mean?
ANSWER 856
"REMA" is one of the Greek words meaning "*word*." It usually refers to "*spoken word*" as it flows from a person's mouth. It comes from REO which means "*to flow*."

REMA and Tongues
QUESTION #857
I went this morning to a church. This pastor was telling the believers that they needed a "REMA." He was referring to speaking in tongues. Is it Scriptural to ask for a "REMA"? Do we need to ask God for this "REMA" in our lives?
ANSWER #857
"REMA" is one of the Greek words for "*word*." It is literally a "*spoken word*." It comes from REO which means "*to flow*." This is why this pastor used it in connection with speaking in tongues. We should not ask God for "REMA" in our lives. The Bible is now complete as of 90 or 100 A.D. I believe that these miraculous sign gifts that God gave in the New Testament before the Bible was completed are no longer God-given gifts. I believe these present manifestations of "*tongues*" are caused by the flesh, by the Devil, or by both.

"Hear" vs. "Understand"
QUESTION #858
I need some help in defending the King James Bible. There are two questions I would like to get help with.

#1. Acts 9:7, and Acts 22:9 I always thought it was like the two different meanings of *"hear"* in English like one is hearing a sound, and the other is hearing with understanding and willingness. Kind of like *"he would not hear of it"* does not mean he did not hear but more he would not listen. Is that correct?

#2. In John 7:8,10 it seems to me that many versions make Jesus lie by leaving out the first *"yet"* in verse 8.

John 7:8 *"Go ye up unto this feast: **I go not up yet unto this feast**; for my time is not yet full come."* (King James Bible)

John 7:8 *"Go ye up unto the feast: **I go not up   unto this feast**; because my time is not yet fulfilled."* (ASV)

John 7:10 *"But when his brethren were gone up, then **went he also up unto the feast**, not openly, but as it were in secret."* (King James Bible)

John 7:10 *"But when his brethren were gone up unto the feast, then **went he also up**, not publicly, but as it were in secret."* (ASV)

I have brought this up to others and they brush it off and try to say that the yet in the last part of the verse has the same effect basically, because the time Jesus is referring to is His time to go to the feast. Is there any way you can help explain this to me in a way to help stand up for the King James Bible?

ANSWER #858

#1. Your understanding of this is correct. The Greek construction of Acts 9:7 indicates that the men only **heard** a sound, but did not distinguish what was said. The Greek construction of Acts 22:9 indicates that those who were with Paul did not **hear** in the sense of *"understand"* what was said.

Acts 9:7 And the men which journeyed with him stood speechless, **hearing a voice**, but seeing no man.

Acts 22:9 And they that were with me saw indeed the light, and were afraid; but they **heard not the voice** of him that spake to me.

#2. This is correct. The Gnostic Critical Greek Text of Westcott and Hort, United Bible Societies (UBS) and Nestle/Aland (NA) all omit the first *"yet."* These false Greek texts are calling the Lord Jesus Christ a liar because in verse 8 He told his half brothers he was not **yet** going up to Jerusalem but in verse 10 he did go up to Jerusalem. Without the first "yet," the Lord Jesus Christ is made out to be a liar. You are correct in this.

Greek Interlinears

QUESTION #859

I have two Interlinear Greek-English New Testaments:
1. the 1972 edition by George Ricker Berry
2. the 1985 2nd Edition by Jay P. Green

Can you tell me if these are reliable books, faithful to the 1611 King James Bible, or if there is a better or preferred Interlinear.

ANSWER #859

I have both of these also. Both of these are helpful in their own way.

Berry uses the King James Bible in the margin which I prefer, but uses the Stephens 1550 Greek text which I do not prefer.

Green uses the Jay Green translation in the margin which I don't prefer, but uses the 5th edition of Beza (1598) and Scrivener's Greek text which I prefer.

Both interlinears help you to identify the Greek word in question and then you can look it up in some other sound Greek lexicon for greater accuracy. As far as I know, as of now, these are the only two interlinears that try to follow the Traditional Greek Text. There are interlinears that follow the Gnostic Critical Greek Text, but I don't recommend them.

Greek Lexicons
QUESTION #860

I really enjoy your website. I have been listening to the Greek classes online. I wanted to know your opinion on the BADG Greek Lexicon. Is it accurate or liberal? I want a professional conservative independent fundamental Baptist opinion, and I know you will give me a straight answer. Are Spiros Zodhiates' Word Study Dictionaries dependable?

ANSWER #860

I have not examined the BADG Greek Lexicon by Bauer and Danker. My preferences for Lexicons are as follows: For the Greek, I prefer the *NEW ANALYTICAL GREEK LEXICON*. For the Hebrew, I prefer the *ANALYTICAL HEBREW LEXICON*. They give you the exact spelling of the words as they occur in the Bible. From that, they give you the root of the word, and you can go to that root and find many useful meanings. I don't use Spiros Zodhiates. He is not to be trusted because he sometimes fights against readings of the Textus Receptus that underlie the King James Bible.

Greek Pronunciation
QUESTION #861

I am reading an article by Chrys C. Caragounis. He attacks Erasmus. He said that it was Erasmus that made up the pronunciation of the Greek language. He said that is there was never an ancient Greek pronunciation and a modern one. Is all this true?

ANSWER #861

I'm not sure. <u>I think Erasmus did give us the Greek pronunciation of Koine New Testament Greek that we use</u>. But there are other developments in the Greek language such as Homeric Greek, classical Greek such as Attic Greek, modern Greek, and many other types of Greek. All of these periods of the developoment of the Greek language had different spellings, different grammatical rules, and different pronunciations.

http://www.biblicalgreek.org/links/pronunciation.php   This is a LINK that gives the history of Greek pronunciation, including Erasmus' influence.

Mark "In" or "On"

QUESTION #862

I am very much a King James Bible only advocate, yet I have been reading recently about the translation in the Textus Receptus clearly stating that the "*mark*" will be "*on*," and not "*in*" the hand or forehead as the King James Bible states. This is confusing to me and is very important to establish the truth in this matter. I have found a couple of instances recently where the following is stated:

> *Notice that the Greek word used to describe the location of the Mark is EPI which means "on" or "over," and not EIS which means "in" or "into."*

I wonder if you could clear this up for me.

ANSWER #862

The two verses in Revelation that concern this are the following:

> Revelation 13:16 "*And he causeth all, both small and great, rich and poor, free and bond, to receive a mark __in__ their right hand, or __in__ their foreheads:*"

> Revelation 14:9 "*And the third angel followed them, saying with a loud voice, If any man worship the beast and his image, and receive his mark __in__ his forehead, or __in__ his hand,*"

<u>In both verses, the prepositions translated "in" are from the same Greek word, **EPI**. Here are the various meanings of EPI</u>:

1909 epi {ep-ee'}

a root; prep

AV - <u>**on 196**</u>, <u>**in 120**</u>, upon 159, unto 41, to 41, misc 338; 895

1) upon, on, at, by, before

2) of position, on, at, by, over, against

3) to, over, on, at, across, against

You can see from this that the King James Bible translates it "*on*" 196 times and "*in*" 120 times, depending on the context. I notice that the NIV, NASV, and NKJV translate it "*on*" rather than "*in*."

The 21st Century King James Bible has "*in*"

The Wycliffe New Testament has "*in*"

So you can see that there is a divergence of opinion on this matter. At least we are certain that the location of the marks are on the foreheads and the right hands. Since "*in*" was used for the Greek preposition, EPI, in 120 cases in the King James Bible, why should it be doubted in these two places in Revelation?

"For" or "Because of"

QUESTION #863

Romans 4:25   "*Who was delivered for our offences, and was raised again for our justification.*"

I usually have phone fellowship with a very dear prayer partner on Sunday afternoons. Recently we got into a discussion concerning Romans 4:25 because her current Sunday School teacher had raised a translation issue. She uses the King James Bible, but I'm not sure which translation he uses. He claimed that where the King James Bible translated "*raised again for our justification,*" the preposition, "*for,*" should be translated "*because of*" according to the Greek. She checked her *Word Studies in the Greek New Testament*. She told me that confirmed the "*because of*" translation, which changes it considerably. Afterwards, I checked my *Interlinear Greek-English New Testament* by George Ricker Berry. I discovered it to be translated "*for.*"

ANSWER #863

The word translated "*for*" in the King James Bible is DIA. Here are some of the various meanings for DIA.

223 **dia** {dee-ah'}

a primary preposition denoting the channel of an act;

  TDNT - 2:65,149; prep

AV - by 241, through 88, with 16, **for 58**, for ... sake 47,

  therefore + 5124 44, for this cause + 5124 14, **because 53**,

  misc 86; 647

1) through

  1a) of place

    1a1) with

    1a2) in

  1b) of time

    1b1) throughout

1b2) during

1c) of means

   1c1) by

   1c2) by the means of

2) through

  2a) the ground or reason by which something is or is not done

   2a1) by reason of

   2a2) on account of

   2a3) **because of for this reason**

   2a4) therefore

   2a5) on this account

From the above statistics, you can see that DIA is translated "*for*" in the King James Bible **58 times**. It is translated "*because*" only **53 times**.

The above are the various meanings of **DIA** which is the word "*for*." From this, it can be clearly seen that both meanings are valid for DIA.

"*Because of*" is one meaning of the English word, "*for*." Note the following sentences.

1. I went to the dentist **for** (because of) my toothache.

2. She wept **for** (because of) sadness.

3. He cried **for** (because of) his father's death.

4. I took my car to the repair man **for** (because of) stalling.

The "*for*" in the first part of the verse is also a translation of **DIA** the same as in the last part of the verse. Interpretations, of course, always vary depending on the context.

---

2 Peter 1:1

QUESTION #864

I was asked recently a difficult question on the presence of the two possessive pronouns in 2 Peter 1:1 in the Scrivener Greek text while the AV translators evidently only saw the one. Since I know that you are very knowledgeable on these matters, I thought that I should check with you. What do you think?

ANSWER #864

2 Peter 1:1 "*Simon Peter, a servant and an apostle of Jesus Christ, to them that have obtained like precious faith with us through the righteousness of* [ ] *God and **our** Saviour Jesus Christ:*"

I would simply note that though two HEMON'S ("*our*") are present in the Textus Receptus Greek, the grammar of our English language does not demand that both be translated. One pronoun, *"our,"* could describe both the words, *"God"* and *"Saviour."*

Proper Greek N.T. Texts
QUESTION #865

[After quoting the Dean Burgon Society's Articles of Faith and a DBS resolution defending the King James Bible and its underlying Hebrew, Aramaic, and Greek Words, the following question was asked:]

Does that mean that you reject all the Greek New Testament manuscripts that have been discovered since 1611 if they do not agree with the Greek New Testament manuscripts which were used by the King James Bible translators in 1611? Can you please tell me what Greek New Testament manuscripts were used in 1611, and why you believe that they are closer to the originals than those Greek New Testament manuscripts that have been discovered since 1611, some of which were written much earlier than those Greek New Testament manuscripts that were known in 1611 ? I have read much of what Dean Burgon and Jack Moorman have written, but haven't been able to figure out the answers to those questions, so I would be grateful for your opinion.

ANSWER #865

The Greek edition most likely used by the King James Bible translators was Beza's 5th Edition of 1598. Only 190 passages out of over 140,500 Greek words in the N.T. were from some other source, according to Dr. Frederick Scrivener's Appendix. These Greek Words go back closer to the original N.T. Greek Words than any other source. The Vatican and Sinai manuscripts and those following this minority of manuscripts were influenced by the Gnostic heresies in Alexandria, Egypt. Because of these heresies, these manuscripts were polluted. You can take any manuscripts you wish. I'll stick to the ones I believe to be preserved by the Lord in over 99% of the manuscript evidence rather than less than 1% of the manuscripts on which the new versions are based. There are many books, articles, and tapes available that give solid evidence for my position on this.

The Moveable Greek "NU"
QUESTION #866

In declining verbs I noticed in the textbook and in the online lecture that the third person plural declension is shown with an ending of OUSI. Why do some include a NU (v) on the end? When, if ever, is that required or appropriate?

ANSWER #866

The final "NU" is sometimes used and sometimes not. That is why it is called a *"movable NU."* http://en.wikipedia.org/wiki/Nu_ephelkustikon is a LINK that gives you the background of this Greek moveable NU.

Greek Questions or Statements

QUESTION #867

Does the Greek language employ an absolute means to know whether a sentence is a declarative or question? The specific example is:

1 Corinthians 6:4, *"If then ye have judgements of things pertaining to things of this life, set them to judge who are least esteemed in the church."*

Some Bible versions make this verse into a question. My question is, how strong is the Greek construction to specify whether this is a declarative statement; and does any justification exist for allowing that this might be a question?

ANSWER #867

http://mylanguages.org/greek_questions.php is a LINK that gives some rules about questions in the Greek language. Sometimes there is a Greek indication of a question, but in this case all such indication is missing. It is an interpreter's choice. I see no reason to make this a question and every reason to leave it as a statement. Here's a list of fifteen translations showing how each of them interpret this verse.

The King James Bible has a statement.
The NIV has a statement.
The 21st Century King James Bible has a statement.
The Young's Literal Translation, has a statement.
The Darby Version has a statement.
The NASV has a question.
The NKJV has a question.
The Message has a question.
The Amplified Bible has a question.
The ESV has a question.
The Contemporary English Version has a question.
The New Century Version has a question.
The Holman Christian Standard has a question.
The Worldwide English New Tetament has a question.
Today's English Version has a question.

CHAPTER VI
QUESTIONS ABOUT THE
HEBREW OLD TESTAMENT

Concubine Cut in 12 Pieces
QUESTION #868

Pastor Waite, I have been reading in Judges and I was just reading chapter 19 verse 29. I don't understand why the man cut his concubine up into 12 pieces, and sent her to all the coasts of Israel? I am not sure if it had something to do with the 12 tribes of Israel, and that is why there was 12 pieces.

ANSWER #868

I believe you are correct that the man sent one piece of the woman's body to each of the 12 tribes of Israel to show them how wicked these homosexual men were. I believe that this rallied Israel to judge these homosexuals and kill them and those who sheltered them as mentioned later in Judges 20:10 and following verses.

"Jehovah" or "LORD God"
QUESTION #869

I have a question about God's name translated in King James Bible as "The LORD God." Our Chinese translated it as "Jehovah" as Darby's Bible, the Young's Literal Translation, the ASV, and the New World Translation. We are not sure if we should keep "*Jehovah*" or change it. Please advise.

ANSWER #869

The King James Bible uses the translation "LORD God" for the Hebrew JEHOVAH ELOHIM in such verses as Genesis 2:4 and 2:5. The King James Bible uses the full word, JEHOVAH, instead of LORD in only the following seven places in the Old Testament.

Genesis 22:14 "*And Abraham called the name of that place **Jehovah**jireh: as it is said to this day, In the mount of the LORD it shall be seen.*"

Exodus 6:3 *"And I appeared unto Abraham, unto Isaac, and unto Jacob, by the name of God Almighty, but by my name JEHOVAH was I not known to them."*

Exodus 17:15 *"And Moses built an altar, and called the name of it Jehovahnissi:"*

Judges 6:24 *"Then Gideon built an altar there unto the LORD, and called it Jehovahshalom: unto this day it is yet in Ophrah of the Abiezrites."*

Psalms 83:18 *"That men may know that thou, whose name alone is JEHOVAH, art the most high over all the earth."*

Isaiah 12:2 *"Behold, God is my salvation; I will trust, and not be afraid: for the LORD JEHOVAH is my strength and my song; he also is become my salvation."*

Isaiah 26:4 *"Trust ye in the LORD for ever: for in the LORD JEHOVAH is everlasting strength:"*

I believe one of the reasons for TRANSLATING the word, *"Jehovah,"* as LORD instead of transliterating it as *"Jehovah,"* was because of the additional space this would have taken in the Hebrew manuscripts. In the New Testament, it is KURIOS HO THEOS. I would NOT advise using Jehovah in the New Testament since it is an Old Testament Hebrew Name.

Jeremiah 10:3-5--Christmas Trees?
QUESTION #870

Am I wrong in my interpretation of Jeremiah 10: 3-5?

"For the customs of the people are vain: for one __cutteth a tree out of the forest__, the work of the hands of the workman, with the axe. They deck it with silver and with gold; they fasten it with nails and with hammers, that it move not. They are upright as the palm __tree__, but speak not: they must needs be borne, because they cannot go. Be not afraid of them; for they cannot do evil, neither also is it in them to do good." (Jeremiah 10:3-5)

It seems that this could be applied to Christmas Trees. If that isn't the case, what is it referring to? Jeremiah 10:2 says *"learn not the way of the heathen."* Couldn't that be applied to bringing trees into our houses to decorate them? Thank you for clarification on these verses.

ANSWER #870

This application and interpretation sounds good to me. This practice mentioned in Jeremiah could be applied to people's practices today with the decoration of *"Christmas trees"* even though the name is not mentioned. It is the use of trees used for heathen worship.

Methusaleh And Noah's Flood
QUESTION #871
My dad mentioned to me that the Bible taught that Methusaleh lived through the flood and then mentioned about Noah. Somehow or another, my dad heard about the teaching in the Septuagint and the confusion over that subject. He said that the Old Testament was mere stories (exaggerated over time) and that the New Testament had more truth. It is obvious that the Septuagint caused confusion for my dad. I would not be surprised that the Septuagint has caused problems for other people also. It was very interesting to get the information from your ministry on the Septuagint to come to understand what had happened to my dad and where the teaching came from that he had heard!

ANSWER #871
Your father was wrong about Methuselah. He died just before the universal flood of Noah came upon the earth. The Greek Septuagint (LXX) translation from the Hebrew has many errors in the chronologies found in Genesis 5 and 10. It cannot be trusted in any area, especially when it differs with the facts stated in the Hebrew text. The years that people lived as noted in the Greek Septuagint are around 1,000 years different than those given in our accurate Hebrew text. That's another reason for rejecting the LXX in any area where there is a conflict.

The Septuagint–B.C. or A.D.?
QUESTION #872
Was the Septuagint (LXX) composed before Christ's time, or was it composed after His time on earth?

ANSWER #872
Though the liberals, the neo-evangelicals, and most fundamentalists today teach that the Septuagint (LXX) was B.C., I believe it was composed in the time of Origen in the 200's A.D. It is true that a few parts of the Old Testament were translated from Hebrew into Greek, no one has ever produced the entire B.C. Old Testament from Genesis through Malachi in the Greek language. Until this has been produced, I cannot believe it existed B.C. Origen's 5th column of his *Hexapla* has the Septuagint (LXX) in its entirety. That is the origin of it rather than its origin being B.C.

Meaning of "Replenish"
QUESTION #873

Why is the word *"replenish"* used in Gen 1:28 and 9:1?   It seems to be saying it had been populated before.

> Genesis 1:28 *"And God blessed them, and God said unto them, Be fruitful, and multiply, and __replenish__ the earth, and subdue it: and have dominion over the fish of the sea, and over the fowl of the air, and over every living thing that moveth upon the earth."*
>
> Genesis 9:1 *"And God blessed Noah and his sons, and said unto them, Be fruitful, and multiply, and __replenish__ the earth."*

ANSWER #873

The prefix, *"re,"* in *"replenish"* does not necessarily mean *"again"* or *"plenish again."* Like the "re" in "refresh" it merely means *"to make fresh,"* so *"replenish"* merely means *"to make full."*   It does not have to mean there was a pre-Adamic creation before Genesis 1. Though it is true that the prefix, *"re"* usually means *"again,"* or *"back,"* there are some exceptions such as Rebuke, record, relief, religion, recluse, or relic. It is true, however, that the Hebrew word, מָלֵא (mālē') clearly means simply *"be full,"* or *"to fill."*

LORD or "Jehovah"
QUESTION #874

Is the printed Name of *"Jehovah"* in various Old Testament translations a *"transliteration"* (letter for letter) or a *"translation"*? I know *"Jehovah"* in many places in the King James Bible is translated as LORD in English.

ANSWER #874

I believe Jehovah is not only a *"transliteration"* (letter for letter) of the Hebrew, but is also the proper pronunciation of that Hebrew word. Some wrongly hold that it should be pronounced YAWEH. However, the vowel pointing in Hebrew is clear that, as it appears in the Hebrew Old Testament, it must be pronounced Jehovah. http://en.wikipedia.org/wiki/Jehova gives some of the background on this.

Meaning of Daniel 11:38
QUESTION #875

I have been studying the book of Daniel. I am having trouble finding an answer to why Daniel 11:38 has a capital "G" for God when the context is about the antichrist.

*"But in his estate shall he honour the **God** of forces: and a god whom his fathers knew not shall he honour with gold, and silver, and with precious stones, and pleasant things."* (Daniel 11:38)

I would appreciate any help on this and any resource that give answers to these types of concerns.

ANSWER #875

As you may know, the capitalization in the Hebrew or Aramaic is left to a translator's interpretation. I agree with you that a small "g" would have been a better interpretation. I don't think we should fault the King James Bible's text or translation here, we might just disagree with the capitalization.

Song of Solomon 2:7
QUESTION #876

I was wondering if you know why the Song of Solomon has been changed and accepted by many in chapter 2:7. Also, who settled the modern King James Bible text? Based on what authority was it settled? AV1611: "till **she** please." Present King James Bible: "till **he** please."

ANSWER #876

I don"t know why it was changed from *"she"* to *"he"* nor on what authority. I know that in the history of the King James Bible, they talk about both the *"she Bible"* and the *"he Bible."* I looked it up in 10 or 15 versions. Many have *"he,"* only one has *"she."* The NIV, the ESV, and others have *"it."*

The *"King James Bible text"* was settled as to its Hebrew, Aramaic, and Greek Words from 1604 to 1611 during the time of its translation. Various words and spellings were modified during seven revisions. The present King James Bible is the 7th edition of 1769.

Sheol and "Grave"
QUESTION #877

In 1 Samuel 2:6, the word, *"grave,"* is used. Does it have the meaning of a literal or just a subterranean place as suggested by Strong?

ANSWER #877

*"The LORD killeth, and maketh alive: He bringeth down to the **grave**, and bringeth up."* (1 Samuel 2:6) The word translated *"grave"* in the King James Bible is SHEOL. The meaning of that word is as follows:

07585 sh@'owl {sheh-ole'} or sh@ol {sheh-ole'}

from 07592; TWOT - 2303c; n f

AV - grave 31, hell 31, pit 3; 65

1) **sheol, underworld, grave, hell, pit**

  1a) the underworld

  1b) Sheol - the **OT designation for the abode of the dead**

    1b1) place of no return

    1b2) without praise of God

    1b3) **wicked sent there for punishment**

    1b4) righteous not abandoned to it

    1b5) of the place of exile (fig)

    1b6) of extreme degradation in sin

According to Luke 16:19-31, there were two divisions in SHEOL. One was the place of paradise for the just. The other was the place of condemnation for the unjust. The New Testament word for this place is HADES.

Lucifer's Position in Heaven

QUESTION #878

*"Thou art the anointed **cherub that covereth**; and I have set thee so: thou wast upon the holy mountain of God; thou hast walked up and down in the midst of the stones of fire."* Ezekiel 28:14

Do you know exactly what Lucifer's position was in heaven? What was he covering?

ANSWER #878

I do not have answers to your questions about the *"**cherub that covereth**."* Since the cherubs *"covered"* the mercy seat, Lucifer might have been one of these cherubs.

"And make one cherub on the one end, and the other cherub on the other end: even of the mercy seat shall ye make the cherubims on the two ends thereof." (Exodus 25:19)

Before his fall, it would appear that Lucifer was the archangel or leading angel in heaven. He was one of the *"sons of God"* or angels spoken of in Job 1:6; 2:1; and 38:7.

The Old Testament Hebrew Text
QUESTION #879
Was the Letteris Masoretic Text used at all in the compilation of the King James Bible? The Letteris was "based" on the Bomberg (Ben Chayyim). I'm trying to find out the sources Max Letteris used in making his "revision."

ANSWER #879
Since the Letteris Text came out in about 1866, this was before the 1881 English Revised Version (ERV). It is assumed to be based on the Bomberg Ben Chayyim Hebrew underlying the King James Bible. We carry a parallel Letteris and King James Bible. I believe it is trustworthy. In the final analysis I believe and teach that the most trustworthy Words are the Hebrew, Aramaic, and Greek Words underlying the King James Bible. If they are slightly different from either Letteris or Ben Chayyim (Bomberg), I take those words to be accurate. I believe there are very few such differences either in Hebrew, Aramaic, or in Greek.

"Watch" or "Hasten"
QUESTION #880
In Jeremiah 1:12, there is the use of "*hasten.*" When I looked it up, as far as the Hebrew, it says it means "*watching over.*" I think of the word "*hasten*" as meaning a speeding up of things. The Hebrew lexicon didn't mention anything to that affect. Could it perhaps mean a quickening action also?

ANSWER #880
In looking at the Oxford English Dictionary Unabridged, it shows that in 1677 and 1686, the meaning #7 of "*watch*" in English was "*retreat into its lair*" or possibly "*hasten to its lair.*" I notice SHAQAD is used 12 times in the King James Bible and only uses "*hasten*" this once; "*watch*" 9 times; "*wake*" once, and "*remain*" once. This clears up the apparent difficulty in the meaning of these terms.

The (LXX)
QUESTION #881
It is not easy to find information on the Internet about the textual criticism of the Old Testament. I believe in the Masoretic Text, but I am looking for answers and counter-arguments to two statements that I received and that I can not answer. These statements are pro-LXX. I am not able to handle these statements. Can you help me? These are the two statements, that

try to show that Septuagint (LXX) existed before Christ:

1. Statement 1:   The Proto-Septuagint text-type is represented at Qumran by manuscripts of Joshua, Samuel and Jeremiah.

2. Statement 2:   Targums are ancient Aramaic translations of the Hebrew scriptures. The Targums are important source documents that can be compared with the Septuagint in terms of their significance for doing text criticism, understanding the history of biblical interpretation, and studying the New Testament use of Hebrew scriptures.

Is it true that they only found Greek Old Testament fragments (before Christ) are some parts of 5 chapters of Deuteronomy?

ANSWER #881

http://en.wikipedia.org/wiki/Textual_criticism is a link that tells about Textual Criticism. I am opposed to Textual Criticism as it has been practiced since its inception. In answer to your questions #1 and #2, let me say the following. If indeed the Septuagint in its entirety (Genesis through Malachi) really existed B.C., let the people who proclaim and believe this allegation produce such a document. Otherwise, let it be dated in the late 200's A. D. in Origen's 5th column of his Hexepla. I am not certain whether there were only fragments of the Old Testament in Greek from parts of five chapters of Deuteronomy. I understand that there were a few parts of books that were translated from Hebrew into Greek from the Old Testament B.C., but not the entire Old Testament. Due to this erroneous dating of the Septuagint (LXX), many false conclusions have been drawn.

CHAPTER VII
QUESTIONS ABOUT
VARIOUS TRANSLATIONS

Romans 8:1 and Romans 8:4
QUESTION #882

Why is the phrase, *who walk not after the flesh, but after the Spirit*, from Romans 8:4 added in Romans 8:1?

ANSWER #882

Here are these two verses:

Romans 8:1 "*There is therefore now no condemnation to them which are in Christ Jesus, who walk not after the flesh, but after the Spirit.*"

Romans 8:4 "*That the righteousness of the law might be fulfilled in us, who walk not after the flesh, but after the Spirit.*"

In answer to your question, the above underlined and bolded words in Romans 8:1 were not "*added*" by the King James Bible as your question suggested. However, these words have been **subtracted** from verse 1 by the false Gnostic Critical Greek Text. The full evidence in the manuscripts for the phrase found in Romans 8:1 is found on page 239 in Dr. Moorman's book, *Early Manuscripts, Church Fathers, and the Authorized Version* (**BFT #3230** @ $20.00 + $7.00 S&H). Stick with the Greek Words underlying the King James Bible and not with the words of the false Gnostic Critical Greek Text favored by your pastor, the Scofield editors, and many others.

Translations in Other Languages
QUESTION #883

If the King James Bible is the only trustworthy English version, how can you trust Bibles translated into other languages other than English. I love the King James Bible and several other newer versions and am an independent Baptist. Thank you and God be with you.

ANSWER #883

In order to trust Bibles translated into other languages, there are at least four requirements that faithful translations other than English should meet: (1) They should be based on the preserved original Hebrew, Aramaic, and Greek Words that underlie the King James Bible. This eliminates your "*several other newer versions*" that you "*love*." (2) They should have competent translators who have a working knowledge of both their own language as well as the Hebrew, Aramaic, and Greek. (3) They should use both the verbal and the formal equivalence translation technique rather than the dynamic equivalence technique used by the "*several other newer versions*" that you "*love*." (4) They should have accurate theology rather than accepting more than 356 false doctrinal passages in the New Testament that are found in the "*several other newer versions*" you "*love*" because of their being based on the false Gnostic Critical Greek Text. If all four of these requirements are met, there can be produced accurate translations into other languages. If the translation fails in any one of these requirements, it could not be termed altogether satisfactory.

"Joshua" and "Jesus"

QUESTION #884

Is there a place in the New Testament where the names of "*Joshua*" and "*Jesus*" are interchanged? According to Strong's Concordance, "*Joshua*" does not appear in the King James Bible. Thanks in advance for your help in the "*Joshua/Jesus*" question.

ANSWER #884

"*Jesus*" is used in reference to "*Joshua*" in the following New Testament verses:

> **Hebrews 4:8** "*For if __Jesus__ had given them rest, then would he not afterward have spoken of another day.*"
>
> **Acts 7:45** "Which also our fathers that came after brought in with **Jesus** into the possession of the Gentiles, whom God drave out before the face of our fathers, unto the days of David;"

This is the transliteration (letter for letter) of the Greek text. In Hebrew, the transliteration (letter for letter) for his name is "*Joshua*." The King James Bible text is correct here for having the name Jesus (IESOUS) though the reference, by interpretation, is to "*Joshua*" of the Old Testament.

Using "Perfect" For Translations

QUESTION #885

I understand the criticism against calling any **translation** "perfect." But if, in 1 Corinthians 13:10, *"that which is perfect is come"* refers to "the Scriptures," wouldn't it make sense to say that we can have a *"perfect"* Bible? By *"perfect,"* I mean accurate, exact, complete--lacking nothing and having nothing unnecessary that has been added. I am aware there may exist grammatical errors, which can be fixed as soon as they are found. I am also aware of polysemy, synonyms, or variants in the Greek or Hebrew. However, I don´t need tongues or visions or dreams to know what God has said. Charismatics often say that their Bible isn´t perfect, so they would logically promote the "gifts." With that definition, would you concur that our RVG Spanish translation is "perfect"?

ANSWER #885

1 Corinthians 13:10's *"when that which perfect is come"* refers to the completed Bible after the book of Revelation was completed. It refers exclusively to the preserved original infallible inerrant and *"perfect"* Hebrew and Aramaic Words of the Old Testament and the Greek Words of the New Testament. It has nothing whatsoever to do with any translation in any language including the King James Bible, the Reina-Valera-Gomez (RVG) Spanish, or any other language translation. In the strictest sense of the word, *"perfect,"* only God and what God does is *"perfect."*

> (Psalm 18:30) *"As for God, his way is **perfect**: the word of the LORD is tried: he is a buckler to all those that trust in him."*
>
> **Meaning 3a** in the *Oxford English Dictionary Unabridged*: *"In the state proper to anything when completed; complete; having all the essential elements, qualities, or characteristics; **not deficient in any particular**."*
>
> **Meaning 4a** (*op. cit.*): *"In the state of complete excellence; **free from any flaw or imperfection of quality; faultless**. But often used of a near approach to such a state, and hence capable of comparison, perfecter (= more nearly perfect), perfectest (= nearest to perfection)."*

As you can see from these two definitions, the word, *"perfect,"* is too strong a word for anything that men or women can produce. It should used to describe what God has produced, namely, His own Hebrew, Aramaic, and Greek Words of the Bible.

The King James Bible, as I mentioned in *Defending the King James Bible* (pp. 198 and 199), the Authorized Version 1611 had at least 23 printed editions containing many imperfections and errors. The King James Bible went through at least seven editions. If the AV in 1611 was *"perfect,"* why was it necessary to have these many editions which changed hundreds of its words? I think *"accurate, true, and faithful"* are proper adjectives to use for the King James Bible. Or, as I have stated it, the King James Bible is *"God's Words kept intact in English."*

As fine as Dr. Humberto Gomez's RVG Spanish Bible is, I do not think it should be called *"perfect."* Consider all the revisions it has gone through. If it were *"perfect,"* it would have needed no revision. I believe *"accurate, true, and faithful"* are proper adjectives to use for the RVG. Or *"God's Words kept intact in Spanish."* I think we must be very sparing and careful in using words that are too high in their meaning. Such words should be restricted to what God does or says.

"That Which Is Perfect"

QUESTION #886

In 1 Corinthians 13:10, in your opinion, does the phrase *"when that which is perfect is come"* refer to the Bible?

ANSWER #886

I believe *"that which is perfect"* (TO TELEION), being neuter, refers to the Book (TO BIBLION) which is also neuter. That Book, the Bible, was completed in 90 or 100 A.D. At that time, all the temporary sign gifts vanished away. They were no longer needed to authenticate the truth of the Christian faith.

Some teach that *"__that which__ is perfect"* refers to the coming of the Lord Jesus Christ in the rapture. While it is true that the Lord Jesus Christ is *"perfect,"* the word for Christ (TO TELEION) is masculine. Since the expression, *"that which is perfect"* (TO TELEION) is neuter, there would be a strong grammatical conflict to refer this to a masculine noun like CHRISTOS. The verse does not say, *"when __He Who__ is perfect is come."* It is not grammatically possible to refer this phrase to the coming of the Lord Jesus Christ in the rapture as some have done.

"It Is I" vs. "I Am"
QUESTION #887
I have been reading material by Craig L. Blomberg. He said that:
"Most English translations hide the Greek by quoting Jesus as saying 'Fear not, it is I.' Actually, the Greek literally says, 'fear not, I am.' (Matthew14:27, Mark 6:50.) *Only John 8:58 has it right."*

I checked Matthew and Mark in the King James Bible but it didn't have "*I am.*" It had "*it is I.*" What you think of this?

ANSWER #887
This is true. Matthew 14:27 and Mark 6:50 in the King James Bible, the NKJV, the NASV, and the NIV, it is translated "*It is I.*" In John 8:58, the King James Bible, the NKJV, the NASV, and the NIV all have "*I am.*" In all three of these verses, the Greek words are EGO EIMI. Literally, it is "*I am.*" But in the context of John 8:58, it is clear that "*I am*" is a title of the Lord Jesus Christ, showing His eternal preexistence and is therefore appropriate. However, in Matthew 14:27, there was a storm. The Lord Jesus Christ was walking on the water. The disciples were afraid and thought it was a spirit. The Lord Jesus Christ identified Himself by the clear English expression of "*It is I.*" In this context, this is the meaning of EGO EIMI. It is the same context in Mark 6:50, a parallel passage. To have translated it in Matthew 14:27 or Mark 6:50 as "*I am,*" would have been confusing. However, it was quite proper to render it "*I am*" in the context of John 5:58.

Young's Literal Translation
QUESTION #888
I've appreciated your work defending the King James Bible over the years. Recently, I met a group of people which claim that God's Word is only faithfully preserved in the original languages. One of them clings to the *Literal Translation Bible* by a Robert Young. Could you give me your take on it? Some of these people despise the King James Bible for translating words that aren't "*literal.*" I can think of several problems with this, but could really use a more studied assessment of the issue.

ANSWER #888
http://www.biblegateway.com/versions/Youngs-Literal-Translation-YLT-Bible/
I just looked at a few verses from this version on the LINK above. It seems to be based on the Textus Receptus. However, though it uses "*thee*"

and "*thou*" in some places, it does not use "*ye*" for the plural of "*you*" such as in John 3:7 rather than "*ye*." It also does away from the word "*born-again*."

> **John 3:7**: "*Thou mayest not wonder that I said to **thee**, It behoveth **you** to be born from above;*"

I don't believe the King James Bible is broken. So why try to fix it? I recommend that you get the *DEFINED KING JAMES BIBLE* which we have printed. It maintains accurate translation of the preserved original Hebrew,

Aramaic, and Greek Words, and defines accurately many uncommon words in the footnotes.

King James 21 & Modern KJV
QUESTION #889

Do you have any thoughts on the *21st Century King James Version* or on the *Modern King James Version*?

http://www.gotquestions.org/21st-Century-King-James-Version-KJ21.html
http://www.av1611.org/kjv/mod_kjv.html

ANSWER #889

The *21st Century King James Version* is fairly close to the King James Bible. I looked at it when it first came out and I was disappointed. We have an analysis of it by various writers. I prefer to remain with the King James Bible. Here are some of the critiques of this version:

BFT #2892-P,122 pp., $12.00, King James 21 & Dr. Ted Letis Analyzed for DBS Women, By Yvonne S. Waite

BFT #2892TP, Cassette, $4.00, King James 21 & Dr. Ted Letis Analyzed for DBS Women, By Yvonne S. Waite

BFT #2887, 6 pp., 2 for $2.00, King James 21 Version Confusion, By David Cloud

BFT #2668,12 pp.,$2.00, 21st Century King James Version–A Brief Critical Review, By D. K. Madden

This work was done by an ecumenical group with people in the National Council of Churches and Roman Catholic church. Before long, in 1998, it was transformed into what they call the *Third Millennium Bible*. That Bible has the Apocrypha in it to appease the Roman Catholics. I would stay away from both of these versions.

The *Modern King James Version* was released in 1962 with several revisions including the latest in 1999. It is the work of Jay P. Green, Sr. and published by Sovereign Grace Publishers in Lafayette, Indiana. Green omits "*thou*" and "*ye*" to distinguish singular and plural "*you*." In my opinion, it should never take the place of the King James Bible.

Defects In the Geneva Bible
QUESTION #890
I was wondering about the Geneva Bible. Should it be used today, or should we stick to the King James Bible?
ANSWER #890
http://en.wikipedia.org/wiki/Geneva_Bible is a link that tells you about the Geneva Bible. It was based on the Textus Receptus, but had many strong Calvinistic notes in it. I am opposed to those notes because I differ strongly with the hyper-Calvinist point of view taught therein. It is true that the Pilgrims brought the Geneva Bible to the USA but changed to the King James Bible very soon. I recommend that all born-again Christians remain with the King James Bible rather than to go over to the Geneva Bible which is now being reprinted and publicized.

Translation Differences Listed
QUESTION #891
Can you point me to a summary document that details the differences between the King James Bible and other English Bibles? I am looking for summary statistics. Can you help me?
ANSWER #891
For objective data on the NIV, I recommend my **BFT #1749-P @ $25.00** + **$10.00 S&H**. You can call with credit card at **856-854-4452** or order online at BibleForToday.org. In this report, I show 8,863 specifics where the NIV has either added, subtracted, or changed the Words of God in some other way compared with the Hebrew, Aramaic, or Greek preserved originals.

For objective data on the NASV, I recommend my **BFT #1494-P @ $15.00 + $10.00 S&H**. In this report, I show over 4,000 specifics where the NASV has either added, subtracted, or changed the Words of God in some other way compared with the Hebrew, Aramaic, or Greek preserved originals.

For objective data on the NKJV, I recommend my **BFT #1442 @ $10.00** + **$8.00 S&H**. In this report, I show over 2,000 specifics where the NKJV has either added, subtracted, or changed the Words of God in some other way compared with the Hebrew, Aramaic, or Greek preserved originals.

Defective English Standard Version
QUESTION #892
How much was paid by the English Standard Version (ESV) people to use the RSV's materials and changing some words?

ANSWER #892

I have in my files a letter from Steven Jones, the President of Bob Jones University, showing that a total of $625,000 was paid to the publishers who published the Revised Standard Version (RSV) in the 1950's. The ESV changed a few words and phrases that were in the RSV in order to make it sound more conservative. For example, they changed "*young woman*" to "*virgin*" in Isaiah 7:14. It still follows the Gnostic Critical Greek Text throughout the New Testament and, as such, has at least 356 passages that are doctrinally heretical. Shame on the many new-evangelicals and even fundamentalists like those at Bob Jones University who use and promote this Bible that is filled with heresy.

NIV Differences

QUESTION #893

I am a Baptist, a user of the King James Bible, and an owner of a *Defined King James Bible.* I am not a pastor, or full-time worker, but I do love to learn. I know the King James Bible comes from the Textus Receptus and the New International Version comes from the Gnostic Critical Greek Text like that of Westcott & Hort. Unfortunately most church people don't understand the difference between the Words of the Textus Receptus and the words of the Westcott & Hort Greek Text.

For example, in John 14:6, the NIV says "*through me*". The King James Bible says "*by me.*" Am I missing anything? How can a layman such as myself find these kinds of differences?

ANSWER #893

The difference between the NIV and the King James Bible in John 14:6 is minor. For major and serious differences, you can consult my book, *Defending the King James Bible,* for 158 important doctrinal differences (**BFT #1594 @ $12.00 + $7.00 S&H**). These are found in Chapter V. For a listing of over 356 important doctrinal differences, you can consult Dr. Jack Moorman's book, *Early Manuscripts, Church Fathers, and the Authorized Version* (**BFT #3230 @ $20.00 + $7.00 S&H**).

Sheol, Hades and Hell

QUESTION #894

I want to start by saying that I regularly read and study the King James Bible translation because I believe it to be the most trusted of Bible translations. However, my pastor recently stated in a Bible study we're doing together that the King James Bible transliterates sheol, hades, etc. poorly as *"hell."* He quotes a few verses from the King James Bible sometimes in his sermons, but mostly he quotes from the New American Standard Version. So my question is this: To the best of your knowledge, what were their reasons for translating the words as they did?

ANSWER #894

The King James Bible "translates" the words "SHEOL" in the Hebrew Old Testament, and "HADES" in the Greek New Testament often as "hell." Other English Bible versions often "transliterate" these words letter for letter rather than "translating" them. Since one section of departed spirits in both

SHEOL and HADES was a place of torment and pain, I believe the translation of "hell" is appropriate to give the meaning of that place of torment.

The Geneva Bible

QUESTION #895

Are you familiar with the 1599 Geneva Bible? It is a real close mirror of the King James Bible as far I can see. What are your thoughts?

ANSWER #895

Yes, I am familiar with the 1599 Geneva Bible. It has many words the same as the King James Bible. It is based on the same Hebrew, Aramaic, and Greek Words as the King James Bible. It has many notes that are not present in the King James Bible. These notes are written from a theologically Calvinist perspective. This was the Bible that the Pilgrims brought to America when they arrived in Plymouth in December of 1620. It took some time for the 1611 King James Bible to be accepted in America. The King James Bible translators consulted the Geneva Bible and other English translations as well as the original Hebrew, Aramaic, and Greek Words when making their English translation. You can see a copy of the entire 1599 Geneva Bible by going to the following LINK: http://www.genevabible.org/Geneva.html

The Scofield Reference Bible

QUESTION #896

I was on your site looking to see if I could purchase a Scofield King James Bible from you. I need one that will have enough room to write notes on the sides of each page. I want to spend my money with you as I hope to support your site. Let me know if I can purchase one of these Bible's from you.

ANSWER #896

Sorry, but we have only the *Defined King James Bible*. Though the Old Scofield King James Bible has many useful notes, because it has many other very seriously erroneous notes such as its repeated questioning of many of the words of the King James Bible that follow the Traditional Received Greek Text, choosing rather to follow the false Gnostic Critical Greek Text instead.

CHAPTER VIII
QUESTIONS ABOUT THE
GREEK SEPTUAGINT (LXX)

The Septuagint (LXX) in General
QUESTION #897

Thank you for your stand for the Words of God. I had a Pastor tell me that Jesus quoted from the Septuagint. This Pastor is from Northland Baptist Bible College and his Church is a member of the Fundamental Baptist Fellowship.(Just to let you know his background). Anyway where can I get information on the Masoretic text compared to the Septuagint?

ANSWER #897

The only two studies we have on the Septuagint so far are: (1) **BFT#2707** (53 pp, @ $5.50 + $4.00 S&H) entitled: *"Did Jesus and the Apostles Quote the Septuagint (LXX)?* It is by Dr. Kirk DiVietro; and (2) **BFT #2161** (58 pp @ $6.00 + $4.00 S&H entitled: *The Septuagint--A Critical Analysis.* It is by Dr. Floyd Jones. These two numbers can be ordered from our BFT WebStore at **http://www.biblefortoday.org/search.asp** if you wish. Both these documents show that the LXX in its entirety was **NOT** in existence B.C., but only in the third century A.D. in the 5th column of Origen's *Hexapla.*

Did the NT Quote the LXX?
QUESTION #898

It doesn't make sense to me that our Lord would quote from the Septuagint. Also, I just found out that originally the King James Bible had marginal notes included in the King James Bible where the translators made notes about the variants. Do you know why later printings of the King James Bible did not include those marginal notes?

ANSWER #898

No it doesn't make sense. In point of fact, I believe that would have been impossible since there was no Greek Septuagint (LXX) of the entire Old Testament until the 200's A.D. It was not even around in the days of our Lord Jesus Christ. If anything, the Greek Septuagint quoted from the Lord Jesus

Christ and the New Testament rather than the other way around. Those apostates, or new evangelicals, or even fundamentalists who teach this falsehood are trying to show that even the Lord Jesus Christ used bad translations, so therefore, we can do so as well today.

It is true that the Authorized Version of 1611 had marginal notes, but only rarely did these notes refer to textual "variants." Most of their notes were alternate possible translations, not alternate texts. They believed they had the right Hebrew, Aramaic, and Greek Words. Again the new translation people try to imply that a great many textual variants were listed. This is false. Of the many marginal notes, very few concerned textual vaiants.

Alleged NT Quotes From the LXX
QUESTION #899
Could you explain why there would be those who teach that the seven quotations (such as v5, etc) in the first chapter of Hebrews are from the Greek Septuagint translation of the Hebrew Old Testament rather than from the Hebrew Old Testament itself? What would make them think that he was quoting from the Greek Septuagint translation rather than from the Hebrew Old Testament itself?

ANSWER #899
I believe that the Greek Septuagint translation of the entire Hebrew Old Testament was not in existence until the 200's A.D. It was the fifth column in Origen's six column Bible called the *Hexapla.* It would have been impossible for Paul to have been quoting from the Septuagint in Hebrews since it was not in existence at that time. The reverse could have been true, that is, the Greek Septuagint might have been quoting Paul in Hebrews.

Since a few words are similar in the Septuagint and in Hebrews, people sometimes wrongly assume they were from each other. A few words are different, however in most cases, showing it is the Hebrew behind it not the Greek. In any case, if anything was quoted from anything, the LXX of the 200's A.D. quoted from Hebrews rather than the other way around.

Sometimes people notice that when the Lord Jesus Christ quotes from an Old Testament passage, it might not exactly match. I believe that the Lord Jesus Christ was the Source and Author of every Word of the Old Testament and the New Testament. As such, He, as the Author, had every right to add, subtract, or change in some other way any Old Testament Hebrew Word in order to serve His purposes of use in the New Testament context.

The Use of the LXX

QUESTION #900

Why do some people use the Septuagint (LXX) and keep referring to it?

ANSWER #900

One reason is that if they can prove that the Lord Jesus Christ and the apostles quoted from the alleged Septuagint (LXX), then they say that the modern translations are all right to use as well. This is false reasoning since there was no Septuagint to quote from until the 200's A.D. when Origen put it into the 5th column of his six column *Hexapla*.

What Determines the LXX's Date?

QUESTION #901

What is the determining factor of when the Septuagint (LXX) was actually made? How can we know for sure when it came into existence?

ANSWER #901

I hold a minority position on this both from the liberal apostates, from the new evangelicals like Dallas theological Seminary, and from fundmentalists like Bob Jones University and others. As I have said many times before, if anyone can show me a complete B.C. Greek Old Testament from Genesis through Malachi (not just a few Greek books or parts of books), I will believe the LXX is B.C. I don't think this is too much to ask of those who believe this. If those who believe in a B.C. LXX cannot produce complete one, I will never believe them. I want proof that no one can give me. The Septuagint (LXX) originated with Origen in Alexandria, Egypt. It is found in the 5th column of his six-column Bible called the *Hexapla*.

Did the Apostles Quote the LXX?

QUESTION #902

Was the Septuagint in existence during time of Apostles? Did they quote from the Septuagint?

ANSWER #902

Origen wrote his *Hexapla* in the 200's A.D. The 5th column of his 6-column work called the *Hexapla* contained the Septuagint. This being so, it would have been impossible for the Apostles to have quoted from a book that didn't exist.

LXX and KJB Marginal Notes
QUESTION #903

It doesn't make sense to me that our Lord would quote from the Septuagint. Also, I just found out that originally the King James Bible had marginal notes included in the King James Bible by which the King James Bible translators made note about variants.

ANSWER #903

I agree with you that it doesn't make sense for the Lord to have quoted from the Septuagint (LXX) even if it had been in existence at the time (which it was not). As far as the original marginal notes in the original King James Bible of 1611, only rarely do they suggest textual "*variants*." Most of their notes were alternate translations, not alternate texts. They believed they had the right text. The new translation people try to imply that the King James Bible 1611 listed a great many textual variants. That is a total falsehood!

Why Not O.T. Hebrew Quotes
QUESTION #904

Could you explain why there would be those who teach that the 7 quotations (such as v5, etc) in the first chapter of Hebrews is from the Septuagint rather than the Old Testament? What would make them think that he was quoting from the Septuagint rather than the Old Testament?

ANSWER #904

Since (as I firmly believe and the evidence shows it) the Greek Septuagint (LXX) was not in completed existence until the 200's A.D. in Origen's 6-column Bible called the *Hexapla*, Paul could not be quoting the Greek Septuagint (LXX) in Hebrews.

Since a few words are similar in the Greek Septuagint (LXX) in the book of Hebrews, and in other places, they wrongly assume that the New Testament quoted the Greek Septuagint. A few words are different, however in most cases, showing it is the Hebrew behind it, not the Greek. In any case, if anything was quoted from anything, it is entirely possible that the Greek Septuagint (LXX) composed in the A.D. 200's quoted from Hebrews rather than the other way around. For a specific study on this very subject, you can get a copy of **BFT #2707**. It is 54 pages for a gift to the BFT of **$5.50 + $7.00 S&H**. The title is: *Did Jesus and the Apostles Quote the Septuagint (LXX)*? It is by Dr. Kirk DiVietro.

N.T. Words Given by the Spirit
QUESTION #905

If those who say that the Greek Septuagint was in existence during the time of Apostles and that an Apostle quoted from the Greek Septuagint in the book of Hebrews, why would he quote from the Septuagint in various places yet did not note the corrections that needed to be made in the Greek Septuagint. If this took place, the writer would be quoting from something represented as genuine Scripture. By not bringing to light the translation problems of the Greek Septuagint, it would be misleading people about the overall validity of the Greek Septuagint.

Rather than saying they were quoting from the Septuagint--could it be that the New Testament writers wrote God's Words in Greek and then later the Septuagint did translate those particular scriptural areas as did the Apostles did say them in Greek rather than the other way around. Why would the Apostles need to quote from the Septuagint since they were writing the inspired Words of God? They had no need to check a translation.

ANSWER #905

Your reasoning is correct. The Apostles, being Jews, knew Hebrew, and living at the time they did also know Greek. What you wrote makes a lot of sense. You have, in effect, answered your own question. The Lord gave them the Words and they did not need to consult any translation.

The KJB's O.T. Source
QUESTION #906

Why did the King James Bible translators use the Masoretic Hebrew translation of the Old Testament and also the Greek Septuagint (LXX)?

ANSWER #906

For the Old Testament, the King James Bible translators followed the Hebrew Words, not the LXX words. Though the KJB translators said some good words (sad to say) about the Septuagint (LXX), they did not follow it for their translation of the King James Bible. As far as the translation accuracy of the Septuagint (LXX), according to the article on the Septuagint found in the *International Standard Bible Encyclopedia* (ISBE), in a few places, it is an accurate translation of the Hebrew Words, but in most places in its Old Testament, it is a very sloppy translation of the Hebrew and should not be relied upon or elevated above the Hebrew Words, as some have done.

CHAPTER IX
QUESTIONS ABOUT
THEOLOGY

Meaning of "Theonomist"
QUESTION #907
What does "*theonomist*" mean?
ANSWER #907
The word, "*theonomist*" comes from the word, "*theonomy*." It comes from two Greek words, THEOS ("God") and NOMOS ("law"). It refers to "God's Law." Those who hold the "*theonomist*" position believe that the Old Testament is still in effect today and should be followed. God is clear on this and refutes it. The theonomists usually hold to an amillennial view of the Bible.

> **Romans 10:4**: "*For Christ is the **end of the law** for righteousness to every one that believeth.*"

> **John 1:17**: "*For **the law** was given by Moses, but grace and truth came by Jesus Christ.*"

Under God's grace in the New Testament, the born-again Christian is not under any part of the law of Moses, not the (1) moral law (nine of which are repeated in the New Testament); not the (2) ceremonial law; and not the (3) civil law.

Abraham's "Seed" & Premillennialism
QUESTION #908
I heard a so-called preacher trying to dismiss the doctrine of premillennialism by saying that "*Christians and the church are the true Jews.*" He gave the following verse to prove this: Galatians 3:29. He added that "*the premillennialists interpret the scriptures literally, so they must take this verse literally.*" Can you interpret for me the above verse?

ANSWER #908

Premillennialism is taught in the Bible. It teaches that the Lord Jesus Christ will return to this earth before He sets up and reigns on this earth for one thousand years of the millennium.

---

*"And if ye be **Christ's**, then are ye **Abraham's seed**, and heirs according to the promise."* (Galatians 3:29)

By no means whatsoever can Christians be called *"true Jews."* This verse does not teach this. The verse means that, if you are genuinely saved and born-again (*"Christ's"*). You belong to the Lord Jesus Christ. You are also *"Abraham's seed"* because, as Abraham had genuine faith in the *"Seed"* Who would one day come into the world to die for everyone's sins, so Christians exercise genuine faith in this same *"Seed."* In that sense, and in that sense alone, they are *"Abraham's seed."* That doesn't make them *"true Jews."* It was a fulfillment of Genesis 22:18:

*"And in thy **seed** shall all the nations of the earth be blessed; because thou hast obeyed my voice."*

This represents our **spiritual** relation to Abraham, not our **physical** relation to Abraham, making us Jews. Christians are not Jews, but born-again and genuinely saved Jews can become Christians. Don't let preachers cause you to deny the truth of premillennialism or to each falsely that genuine Christians are *"true Jews."* Christians are Christians, not Jews, true or otherwise.

"It Is Finished"

QUESTION #909

I am teaching the Sunday School class this Sunday. The subject is *"death."* I want to include in the message a brief overview of the spiritual significance of the words *"It is finished"* which the Lord Jesus Christ spoke from the cross. I realize that an entire series of messages could be, and probably have been, developed on these words. I am trying to fill about ten minutes of the message with this subject.

ANSWER #909

The form of the Greek word used for the phrase, *"it is finished"* is TETELESTAI. It is the perfect tense of TELEO. The meaning of the word is below. When the Lord Jesus Christ uttered those final words, here are some of the things that were *"finished"*:

1. The work of redemption for those who genuinely trust the Lord Jesus Christ as their Saviour Who died died for their sins.
2. The law of Moses as to what Christians should not follow.

3. The method of any works that could bring salvation.
4. The end of any other sacrifices like the Mass that the Roman Catholic Church observes daily.
5. The end of being sent to the Lake of Fire in Hell for anyone who has genuinely trusted the Lord Jesus Christ as their Saviour.

Here are some of the meanings of TELEO.

5055 **teleo** {tel-eh'-o}

from 5056; TDNT - 8:57,1161; v

AV - finish 8, fulfil 7, accomplish 4, pay 2, perform 1, expire 1, misc 3; 26

1) **to bring to a close**, to finish, **to end**

  1a) passed, finished

2) to perform, execute, complete, **fulfil**, (so that the thing done corresponds to what has been said, the order, command etc.)

  2a) with special reference to the subject matter, to carry out the contents of a command

  2b) with reference also to the form, to do just as commanded, and generally involving the notion of time, to perform the last act which completes a process, **to accomplish**, fulfil

3) to pay

  3a) of tribute

"*It is finished or paid*" John 19:30

The Meaning of "Theology"
QUESTION #910

Does "*theology*" come from THEO ("God") and LOGY ("word"). Could this mean "word of God" or studying God's word?

ANSWER #910

The word, "*theology*," comes from two Greek words, THEOS ("God") plus LOGOS ("word"). It has always had the meaning of the study about God and God's doctrines which are taught in the Bible.

The Kingdom of God
QUESTION #911

I heard a preacher say; "*the kingdom of God is inaugurated. That's where we as believers are. But this kingdom is not consummated yet.*" Is his saying it right?

ANSWER #911

I make a distinction between the *"kingdom of God"* and the *"kingdom of heaven."* The *"kingdom of God"* is now composed of all truly saved born-again people. The *"kingdom of heaven"* will fully be in effect when the Lord Jesus Christ returns after the rapture and the seven-year tribulation in the 2nd phase of His second coming. At that time, He will set up His thousand-year reign on this earth called the millennium.

Doctrinal Statement Analyzed

QUESTION #912

I've copied some of the points of the doctrinal statement of a school below. Please answer briefly what you think about some of these doctrinal statements.

ANSWER #912

Here are a few defects I can see in some of this school's doctrinal statement. My comments are **underlined** below and put in **bold**. My comments are followed by my initials, "**DAW**." I would personally be uncomfortable recommending this school until I found answers to some my questions below.

1. *". . . who will one day return in a visible, personal, and bodily form as the glorified Lord of Lords and Judge of all mankind to receive His Church unto Himself at a time the Father has reserved to Himself alone."*

There is no mention of the rapture of the genuinely saved people before the seven-year tribulation which follows. DAW

2. *"We believe in only one true and living God, the Creator and Sustainer of all things, who is infinite, eternal, unchanging, and is revealed to us as **the Father, the Head of the Trinity,** into whose hands finally the Kingdom shall be given up."*

The use of *"the Father, the Head of the Trinity"* is strange language. There is no mention of the other Members of the Trinity by Name. DAW

3. *"One God who is Father, Son, & Holy Ghost"*

This could be interpreted as *"modalism,"* that is, the Father, Son, & Holy Ghost are one Person instead of three Persons and one God. DAW

4. *We believe God the Father, God the Son, God the Holy Spirit are three in One.*

This again could be interpreted as *"modalism,"* that is, all three Persons are just one Person. DAW

5. *The Scriptures: We believe that the Bible is the Word of God and is the absolute authority in determining the faith and practice of God's people.*

We affirm that the sixty-six books of the Bible are inerrant, divinely and uniquely inspired, and are given to mankind as the Spirit of God inspired them. These Scriptures are divinely intended for personal study through the guidance of the Holy Spirit.

There is no mention of which Hebrew, Aramaic, or Greek Words they hold to, or which English translation they uphold. DAW

6. "*. . . given in expectation of His imminent return. We believe in the rapture of the Church and the pre-millennial return of Christ with His Church to establish His Kingdom on earth.*"

Once again, there is no mention of the seven-year tribulation period that follows the rapture, and precedes the millennium. Perhaps they do not believe in such a tribulation. DAW

God As A Trinity
QUESTION #913
What is meant when people say that God is a "*Trinity*"?
ANSWER #913

Though the word, "*Trinity*," does not appear in the Bible, it is a word that conveys what is taught in the New Testament that the God of the Bible is "*Triune*," that is, though He is One God, He exists in three Persons, God the Father, God the Son, and God the Holy Spirit. These three Persons are co-equal, co-powerful, and co-eternal. It is a sad thing that the Trinity has been and is denied by Herbert W. Armstrong and his followers, as well as by many other heretical groups.

Here are a few of the verses that teach about God as a Trinity very clearly. They show that the God of the Bible is One God, Who exists in Three separate and distinct Persons.

Matthew 28:19 "*Go ye therefore, and teach all nations, baptizing them in **the name** of the **Father**, and of the **Son**, and of the **Holy Ghost**:*"

Matthew 3:16-17 "*And **Jesus**, when he was baptized, went up straightway out of the water: and, lo, the heavens were opened unto him, and he saw the **Spirit of God** descending like a dove, and lighting upon him: And lo a **voice from heaven**, saying, This is my beloved Son, in whom I am well pleased.*"

Mark 1:9-11 "*And it came to pass in those days, that **Jesus** came from Nazareth of Galilee, and was baptized of John in Jordan. And straightway coming up out of the water, he saw the heavens opened, and **the Spirit like a***

dove descending upon him: And there came **a voice from heaven**, saying, Thou art my beloved Son, in whom I am well pleased."

Luke 3:21-22 "Now when all the people were baptized, it came to pass, that **Jesus** also being baptized, and praying, the heaven was opened, And **the Holy Ghost** descended in a bodily shape like a dove upon him, and **a voice came from heaven**, which said, Thou art my beloved Son; in thee I am well pleased."

Galatians 4:4 "But when the fulness of the time was come, **God** sent forth his **Son**, made of a woman, made under the law, To redeem them that were under the law, that we might receive the adoption of sons. And because ye are sons, **God** hath sent forth the **Spirit** of his **Son** into your hearts, crying, Abba, **Father**."

John 16:12-15 "**I** have yet many things to say unto you, but ye cannot bear them now. Howbeit when he, the **Spirit** of truth, is come, he will guide you into all truth: for he shall not speak of himself; but whatsoever he shall hear, that shall he speak: and he will shew you things to come. He shall glorify **me**: for he shall receive of **mine**, and shall shew it unto you. All things that the **Father** hath are **mine**: therefore said I, that he shall take of **mine**, and shall shew it unto you."

John 15:26 "But when the **Comforter** is come, whom I will send unto you from the **Father**, even the **Spirit** of truth, which proceedeth from the **Father**, he shall testify of **me**:"

What Does Ontological Mean?

QUESTION #914

Is it doctrinally correct to say that, "*the problem of sin in man is Ontological rather than moral*"? Is it really "*ontological*"?

ANSWER #914

The word comes from the Greek verb "*to be*" which is EIMI. ON is a participle and ONTOS is a form of the participle. ON is about "*being.*" The "*ontological argument for the existence of God*" is taken from the fact of our own "*being.*" If we have "*being*" there must have been some force Who also had "*being*" in order to give us "*being.*" Though this argument has been used to prove God's existence, it is not necessary, nor is it adequate. God's existence must be established by faith, not by logical reasoning or "ontology."

"*Ontology*" has been defined as: "*The metaphysical study of the nature of being and existence.*" I've never heard that the "*problem of sin in man*" was "*ontological.*" The Bible teaches clearly that "*sin*" was inherited because of the "*sin*" of Adam in the garden of Eden (Romans 5:12).

Romans 5:12 "*Wherefore, as by one man sin entered into the world, and death by sin; and so death passed upon all men, for that all have sinned:*"

The Bible teaches that "*sin in man*" is "*genetic,*" not "*ontological.*"

Differing On Theology
QUESTION #915

I am discussing with a person about various subjects such as the King James Bible, Biblical theology, Lucifer, eternal Hell, and other things. He differs with me on these and other subjects. What do you think I should do with this person?

ANSWER #915

I disagree with every single objection this man makes against the King James Bible and Biblical theology--from Lucifer to eternal Hell. I believe any argument you begin to make on any of his points would bog you down for ever. It doesn't seem that he is interested in the least in changing his heretical viewpoints. I believe your time is too valuable to waste on a man who is not interested in truth or changing his mind on any of his points. You must make up your own mind on this, but if I were you, I would simply write him and say something like this: "*We must agree to disagree on your points of view against the King James Bible and its doctrines.*"

What Does "Angel" Mean?
QUESTION #916

I've been reading this book where it says that when the Bible talks about "*angels,*" it is talking about men. It says that "*angel*" just means "*messenger.*" I always thought angels were supernatural beings, not "*men*" or just "*messengers.*" What is your understanding on this?

ANSWER #916

Hebrews 13:2 "*Be not forgetful to entertain strangers: for thereby some have entertained angels unawares.*"

The Greek word, AGGELOS, literally means "*messenger.*" Whether it is a human messenger or a Heavenly messenger depends on the context. I believe this would refer back to some of the Old Testament incidents.

Abraham didn't know his visitors were "*angels*," telling him of the destruction of Sodom, for example. They appeared as men. Samson's parents didn't seem to know that an "*angel*" told them of the birth of their son. There are other examples as well. Lot, while in Sodom, was visited by "*men*" who were really "*angels*" who drove away the homosexuals.

QUESTION #917

1 Corinthians 11:19 "*For there must be also **heresies** among you, that they which are approved may be made manifest among you.*"

Can you tell me what "*heresies*" means in this verse? I have "*errors*" in one of my King James Bibles instead of for "*heresies*." Which translation is right?

ANSWER #917

The word, "*heresies*," should be retained in every King James Bible because that is the word that occurs in the 1611 original edition. It is not a "*translation*" but a "*transliteration*" (letter for letter). It comes from the Greek word, HAIRESIS, which comes from the verb, HAIREO, meaning "*to hold or to choose*."

139 <u>hairesis</u> {hah'-ee-res-is}
from 138; TDNT - 1:180,27; n f
AV - sect 5, heresy 4; 9
1) act of taking, capture: e.g. storming a city
2) choosing, choice
3) <u>that which is chosen</u>
4) a body of men following their own tenets (sect or party)
   4a) of the Sadducees
   4b) of the Pharisees
   4c) of the Christians
5) <u>dissensions arising from diversity of opinions and aims</u>

The various "*heresies*" or holdings of doctrines that are not true must be made clear so that those who hold the truth will either remove those who hold false doctrines, or else depart from those who hold these errors. Having these "*heresies*" and false doctrines exposed to view, makes the truth clear, by way of contrast. The heretics should be made to leave the churches so that the truth can be maintained.

Assurance of Salvation
QUESTION #918

Pastor I have some problem with coming to rest on my salvation. I know that it is not of works:

> **Romans 4:5** "*But to him that __worketh not__, but believeth on him that justifieth the ungodly, his faith is counted for righteousness.*"

It is a gift of God that we accept by faith:

> **Ephesians 2:8** "*For by grace are ye saved through faith; and that not of yourselves: it is the gift of God:*"

We cannot lose that salvation:

> **John 3:36a** "*__He that believeth on the Son hath everlasting life__: and he that believeth not the Son shall not see life; but the wrath of God abideth on him.*"

I'm quite confused, though. The idea of going to Hell for my own sins really worries me.

ANSWER #918

The verses you gave are clear. The only way you, or any of us, can "*rest on our salvation*" is confidently to **believe** every one of those verses that God Himself has given us. Our salvation does not "*rest*" on our feelings, but on faith in the facts God gives us in His Words. It "*rests*" on our (1) genuinely believing we are sinners, (2) genuinely believing that the Lord Jesus Christ died for our sins and can save us from Hell, and (3) then genuinely receiving the Lord Jesus Christ as our Saviour. If you don't **believe** these things, you definitely will be going to "*Hell*" for all eternity.

The Sin Unto Death
QUESTION #919

We've encountered two problems with the following verse.

> **1 John 5:16** "*If any man see his brother sin a sin which is not unto death, he shall ask, and he shall give him life for them that sin not unto death. There is a __sin unto death__: __I do not say that he shall pray for it__.*"

> **1 John 5:17** "*All unrighteousness is sin: and there is a __sin not unto death__.*"

1. What do the words, "*sin unto death*" mean? Does it mean "a sin that brings death," "a sin that causes death," or some other meaning?

2. Also, what do these words mean: "*That he should pray for it.*"? What is the "*it*"? Does it refer to death? to sin? or to the life of the sinful person"?

ANSWER #919

1.   1 John 5:16-17 I believe the "*sin unto death*" means a sin which was committed by a Christian that leads to his or her physical death brought about by the judgment of God.

2.   1 John 5:16   Since HE HARMATIA ("*sin*") is feminine and EKEINES ("*it*") is feminine, I believe the "*it*" refers back to the "*sin.*" God tells us that we are not to pray for that "*sin unto death.*" God will judge that person and take him or her Home to Heaven. No amount of prayer will avail in that case.

Meaning of "Eat" and "Drink"

QUESTION #920

John 6:53 "*Then Jesus said unto them, Verily, verily, I say unto you, Except ye __eat__ the flesh of the Son of man, and __drink__ his blood, ye have no life in you.*"

John 6:54   "*Whoso __eateth__ my flesh, and __drinketh__ my blood, hath eternal life; and I will raise him up at the last day.*"

What do these verses mean? Does this mean physically "*__eating__*" Jesus' flesh and "**drinking**" His blood?

ANSWER #920

I think it is important to understand the various meanings of the Greek and English words for "*eat.*"

In this context, I have always interpreted the meaning of "*eat*" and "*drink*" as "*to appropriate, to make it a part of you,*" just as you do when you "*eat*" food or "*drink*" water. It becomes a part of you. In this case, you must appropriate the Lord Jesus Christ by genuinely believing in the Lord Jesus Christ, and truly accepting Him as Saviour as the basis for a person's eternal life. It certainly does not refer to the Roman Catholic error of the Mass. It is clearly a figurative use of "*eat,*" and "*drink,*" not a literal use. The Lord Jesus Christ would have been guilty of advocating unthinkable cannibalism of His own body and blood if He were to have meant His words to be taken literally.

The Law of Moses For Today

QUESTION #921

Do you feel that born-again Christians today should be made to keep the Old Testament law?

ANSWER #921

I do not feel that genuinely born-again Christians are under any of the three divisions of the Mosaic Law. They are free from the (1) ceremonial law,

(2) the civil law, and (3) the moral law (except that part that is repeated in the New Testament).   On the contrary, we are under the commands and obligations that are taught us in the New Testament.

Romans 10:4 *"For Christ is the **end of the law** for righteousness to every one that believeth."*

But born-again Christians should be diligent in studying and reading the Old Testament because of the purposes mentioned in the following verse:

Romans 15:4 *"For whatsoever things were written aforetime were **written for our learning**, that we through **patience** and **comfort** of the scriptures might have **hope**."*

Saved People in the Millennium
QUESTION #922

Are we sure that only those who are saved will enter into the Millennium? Will only saved souls be present for those 1000 years?

ANSWER #922

Only those who are genuinely saved will enter the Millennium.   They will come back with the Lord Jesus Christ after the seven-year tribulation. At the battle of Armageddon the Lord Jesus Christ will slay all the multitudes who will be gathered in that battle near Jerusalem. Probably the judgment of the nations will take place where the sheep nations and the goat nations will be divided. It appears that only the sheep (or saved) people will then enter the Millennium.

However, during the Millennium itself there will be many babies born. If they do not genuinely trust the Lord Jesus Christ a their Saviour, they will be lost. At the end of the Millennium, Satan will be loosed and many unsaved will follow him in the final battle. At the end of the Millennium, the Lord Jesus Christ will judge all the lost at the great white throne judgment.

CHAPTER X
QUESTIONS ABOUT
CALVINISM

Calvinism's TULIP Summary
QUESTION #923
You said you believed the "L"for "Limited atonement" of the TULIP used by the hyper-Calvinists was heretical. How about the "T," "U," "I," and "P"? Do you think those points of Calvinism are also heretical?

ANSWER #923
Depending on how they are defined, the only parts of the Calvinists' five points that I believe to be Biblical are the "T" and the "P."

"T" should not be defined as "total inability" as the Calvinists define it. If it is defined as "total depravity," it would be Biblical.

If the "P" is defined as the "*preservation*" and eternal security of the born-again Christians, it would be Biblical. But many Calvinists define it as the "*perseverance*" of the saints, as though they had to hang on in order to be saved, rather than possessing eternal life once the person is born-again.

I do not believe the "U" as "*unconditional election*" of just a special "*elect*" group to be saved is Scriptural.

Nor do I believe in the Calvinists' "I" or in "*irresistible grace*." If grace were "*irresistible*," no one would be able to resist the gospel message and God then would save all people.

Various Materials On Calvinism
This is a very complex subject that cannot be answered simply. Here are some of the materials on Calvinism that go into all aspects of this complicated philosophy. We carry them in our Bible For Today ministry. Here are the BFT numbers, the gift prices, and the descriptions of the materials. Just add the cost for shipping and the handling (S&P).

#1149/5 Cassette $4.00   Bible & Finished Work (Unlimited Atonement) by Dr. D. A. Waite

#0317   Cassette $4.00   Calvinism's 'Limited Atonement' Refuted By Dr. D. A. Waite

#0596 42 pp. $3.00   Calvinism's Error Of "Limited Atonement" by Dr. D. A. Waite

#1207 4 pp. 2/$1.50   Calvinist Or Biblicist? By Dr. E. R. Jordan

#1346 140 pp. $8.00   Calvinistic Paths Retraced by Rev. Samuel Fisk

#0354 151 pp. $7.50   The Death Christ Died--Unlimited Atonement, by Dr. Robert Lightner

#0983 5 pp. $1.50   Did Christ Die For All Men? by Rev. George Zeller

#0586 22 pp. $2.00   Did Christ Die For All? by Sam Telloyan

#0383 62 pp. $3.00   Elected To Heaven Or Hell? by Dr. Oliver B. Greene

#0185 195 pp. $12.00   Election and Predestination by Rev. Samuel Fisk

#0163 23 pp. $2.50   An Examination of T.U.L.I.P. by D. Robert L. Sumner

#0799 24 pp. $2.50 Five-Point Calvinism & the Inconsistency Of the Four-Point Position by Rev. Samuel Fisk

#2812 34 pp. $3.50   Four Implications of Calvinism by Rev. Mark Huss

#2103 C $4.00   God's Love For Us--A Study Of Unlimited Atonement by Dr. D. D. Champeon

#0984 6 pp. $1.50   God's Willingness-Man's Unwillingness   by Rev. George Zeller

#2827 9 pp. $1.50   Hyper-Calvinism in the Light of Calvin by Dr. Jeffrey Khoo

#2332 284 pp. $12.00   Inside The Tulip Controversy--Calvinism Rebuked & Revisited   by Rev. Kent Kelly

#0367 16 pp. $2.00   Must Baptists Be Extreme Calvinists?   by Dr. Robert L. Sumner

#1396   118 pp. $7.00   Not Chosen To Salvation--Answer To Nettleton's Book   by Dr. Max Younce

#2029 475 pp. $19.00   Other Side Of Calvinism--Documentation Against It by Dr. L. M. Vance

#2605 Cassette $4.00   Predestination As Taught in Scripture   by Pastor Carl D. Drexler

#2592 32 pp. $1.50   Predestination--Biblical Teaching vs. Hyper-Calvinism by James Moffatt

#0141 19 pp. $2.00   Salvation By Grace Through Faith (Eph. 2:1-10) by Dr. D. A. Waite

#1578 1 page 8/$1.50   Suggested Description Of A "Hyper-Calvinist" by Dr. G. Archer Weniger

#2030 16 $1.50   T.U.L.I.P.--Heresy (False Teaching) Of John Calvin by Dr. E. Gamtrell

#0698 6 pp 3/$1.50   What's Wrong With 5-Point Calvinism by Rev. Paul Freeman

The "Limited Atonement" Heresy
QUESTION #924
How do you refute the "L" (Limited atonement) in the TULIP of Calvinism?

ANSWER #924
I wrote a book which refutes "*Limited atonement*." The full book can be found at http://www.biblebelievers.net/Calvinism/kjcalvn4.htm The title of the book is *Calvinism's Error of Limited Atonement* (**BFT #596 @ $6.00 + $3.00 S&P**). I will list here only the TABLE OF CONTENTS so you can see what is involved in the book.

LIMITED ATONEMENT DEFINED

LIMITED ATONEMENT REFUTED BY THE SCRIPTURES

Isaiah 53:5-6 Refutes Limited Atonement

Matthew 11:28 Refutes Limited Atonement

John 1:29b Refutes Limited Atonement

John 3:14 Refutes Limited Atonement

John 3:18 Refutes Limited Atonement

Romans 5:6 Refutes Limited Atonement

2 Corinthians 5:19 Refutes Limited Atonement

1 Timothy 2:5-6 Refutes Limited Atonement

Hebrews 2:9 Refutes Limited Atonement

2 Peter 2:1 Refutes Limited Atonement

1 John 4:14 Refutes Limited Atonement

1 John 2:2 Refutes Limited Atonement

LIMITED ATONEMENT REFUTED BY THE BIBLE'S TERMS FOR
RECEPTION OF SALVATION

The Terms of John 1:12 Refute Limited Atonement

The Terms of John 3:16 Refute Limited Atonement

The Terms of John 3:17 Refute Limited Atonement

Other Verses Among Many Others Whose Terms Refute Limited Atonement

THEOLOGIANS WHO OPPOSE LIMITED ATONEMENT

JOHN CALVIN MODIFIED HIS POSITION AND FAVORED AN UNLIMITED ATONEMENT!

John Calvin Witnesses for Unlimited Atonement - Commentary on Mark 14:24

John Calvin Witnesses for Unlimited Atonement - Commentary on Romans 5:18

John Calvin Witnesses for Unlimited Atonement - Last Will And Testament

CONCLUSIONS

I stand **with** the Bible and **against** any man or philosophy that contradicts the Bible in any point, (including limited atonement) well-meaning as they might be. We will just have to agree to disagree on these and other matters.

Against Spurgeon and Edwards

QUESTION #925

I assume you have great respect for Charles Haddon Spurgeon and Jonathan Edwards. These two preachers and writers, among many others, were very strong defenders of five point Calvinism. Why do you dare stand against them?

ANSWER #925

I stand against any man or system that departs from the clear teachings of the Bible, including Spurgeon and Edwards. As I have explained in a previous question (**#923**), the only part of the five points that I believe to be Biblical are the "T" and the "P" if they are defined accurately.

Biblical Election

QUESTION #926

I have a special request from you. Would you please tell me your position on "*election*"?

ANSWER #926

I believe the Lord Jesus Christ died for the sins of every person who ever lived throughout the entire world, past, present, and future, not just for the "*elect*." I believe in "*election*" because the Bible speaks of it. I believe in a "*corporate election*." That is, in eternity past, God chose a Body, the Church, composed of those who would one day genuinely accept the Lord Jesus Christ as their Saviour and thereby become born-again people.   When people genuinely receive the Lord Jesus Christ as their Saviour and are saved, they become members of that corporate Body which was chosen from before the foundation of the world.

Meaning of "Bought Them"

QUESTION #927

2 Peter 2:1 *"But there were false prophets also among the people, even as there shall be false teachers among you, who privily shall bring in damnable heresies, even denying the Lord that **bought them**, and bring upon themselves swift destruction."*

2 Peter 2:1 shows us that the false teachers that the Lord "***bought***" (Aorist tense and Active Voice in Greek) denied the Lord and brought themselves destruction.   What does "***bought them***" mean in this verse?

ANSWER #927

In 2 Peter 2:1, the words, *"bought them"* indicate that the Lord Jesus Christ died for the sins even of those false teachers.   The Bible teaches clearly that He died for the sins of everyone who ever lived.   It does **not** mean that these false teachers have genuinely accepted and received the Lord Jesus Christ as their Saviour.   But it does teach that He died for their sins.   The verse does not teach universalism, but it does teach the unlimited atonement made by our Saviour just as many other Bible verses teach.

CHAPTER XI
QUESTIONS ABOUT
GAIL RIPLINGER

DBS's Position on Gail Riplinger
QUESTION #928
I was taken aback by Mrs. Waite's exposer of Gail Riplinger's previous marriages and divorces. What is the DBS's position on her?
ANSWER #928
Gail Riplinger believes that the King James Bible was *"given by inspiration of God."* The Dean Burgon Society (DBS) considers this to be a heretical position.   She also minimizes, discounts, and really trashes the Hebrew, Aramaic, and Greek Words underlying the King James Bible that God Himself gave to us.   She does not think they are necessary--the King James Bible is all she needs or believes in. For her, the King James Bible has supplanted God's own Hebrew, Aramaic, and Greek Words. There are many other heresies and lies that she believes in. Here are some of the books we have on her errors.

Materials On Gail Riplinger
From Our BFT Catalog 2012
BFT #3464, 126 pp.,$13.00, A WARNING!! On Gail Riplinger's King James Bible & Inspiration HERESY, Dr. D. A. Waite

BFT #3477, 146 pp., $13.00, Who Is Gail Riplinger?--A Warning For God's Sheep, Aletheia O'Brien

BFT #3479, 108 pp., $11.00, The Messianic Claims Of Gail A. Riplinger, Dr. Phil Stringer

BFT #4011, 126 pp., $13.00, Gail A. Riplinger's Occult Connections, Dr. Phil Stringer

BFT #4018, 4 pp, 2/$1.00, Does Gail Riplinger Have A Right To Sue Those Who Disagree?, Dr. Phil Stringer

BFT #4018PDF, 4 pp., $7.00, Gail Riplinger Is Wrong To Sue Baptists, Dr. Phil Stringer

BFT #4019, 2 pp., 4/$1.00, Gail Riplinger Suing Baptists, Dr. Phil Stringer

BFT #4019PDF, 2 pp., $7.00,Gail Riplinger Is Wrong To Sue Baptists #2, Stringer, Dr. Phil

BFT #4020,3 pp., 3/$1.00,Gail Riplinger Did Threaten To Sue Dr. & Mrs. D. A. Waite, Stringer, Dr. Phil

BFT #4020PDF, 3 pp.,$7.00,Gail Riplinger's Threat To Sue, Williams, Dr. H. D.

BFT #4021,22 pp., $2.50, Gail Riplinger Refuted In Various *BFTUPDATES* (2009--2010), Yvonne S. Waite

BFT #4021PDF, 22 pp., $7.00, Gail Riplinger Answered In *BFTUPDATES*, Yvonne S. Waite

Why Oppose Gail Riplinger?
QUESTION #929
What is the story on Gail Riplinger? Why are you against her positions?
ANSWER #929
The title of one of Gail Riplinger's attack books is *"TRAITORS."* By this epithet, she has included the following people, organizations, literature, a DVD, and various positions as *"traitors"*:

A. PEOPLE
1. Pastor D. A. Waite, Th.D., Ph.D.
2. Mrs. Yvonne S. Waite
3. D. A. Waite, Jr.
4. Dr. H. D. Williams
5. Dr. Kirk DiVietro
6. Dr. Phil Stringer
7. Dr. Maurice Robinson
8. David W. Cloud
9. Mr. Chris Pinto
10. Dr. Frederick Scrivener
11. Theodore Beza
12. Misrepresented Dr. Robert Barnett

B. ORGANIZATIONS
1. The Dean Burgon Society, Incorporated
2. The Bible For Today, Incorporated
3. The Bible For Today Baptist Church

C. LITERATURE
1. *The Defined King James Bible*
2. *The Doctored New Testament*

3. *The Bible For Today UPDATE*
D. A DVD
    A LAMP IN THE DARK--A VISUAL HISTORY OF THE BIBLE
E. POSITIONS SHE IS AGAINST
    ✓ 1. Those who believe the King James Bible is the only accurate, faithful, and true translation from the Hebrew, Aramaic, and Greek Words, but do not believe it is *"given by inspiration of God,"* *"inspired by God,"* *"God-breathed,"* or *"inspired"* in any sense whatever.
    ✓ 2. Those who believe God breathed-out and inspired His Words only in Hebrew, Aramaic, and Greek, rather than in English, Spanish, French, Italian, German, Russian, Chinese, Japanese, or in any other language translations made by men.
    ✓ 3. Those who believe that **only** the original Words given by God in Hebrew, Aramaic, and Greek can be called *"given by inspiration of God,"* *"inspired by God,"* *"God-breathed,"* or *"inspired"* in any sense whatever.

The details of Gail Ludwig Latessa Kaleda Riplinger's lies, misrepresentations, misstatements, distortions, perversions, equivocations, prevarications, fibs, and fabrications will be answered fully at a later time. I just wanted you to be aware of this scurrilous booklet she is now circulating and intends to publish by other means soon.

Inspiration and the KJB
QUESTION #930
Last week, I contacted AV Publications to ask why Gail Riplinger was attacking the Waites? The person I spoke with would not respond to my question even after I stated that it was wrong for believers to go to law against other believers. The individual I spoke to was an employee of the organization so she was not at liberty to say why. But instead, she sent me the attached 61-page copy of Mrs. Riplinger's 61 page document. There is something, however, that troubles me and that is Mrs. Riplinger's claim that you do not believe the King James Bible is inspired, inerrant and infallible. In fact, her claims suggest that she does and that you have in the past opposed members of the Dean Burgon Society who believe that it is. So I simply ask you, what do you believe?

ANSWER #930
We must divide on this subject. The 61-pages sent to you by Gail Riplinger has many, many serious errors and untruths. I believe firmly that the King James Bible is the only faithful, true, and accurate English translation in

existence, but it was **not** "*given by inspiration of God*," "*inspired of God*," "*verbally inspired*," "*God-breathed*" or "*inspired*" in any sense of that word. To use any of these five terms about any translation (including the King James Bible), makes you able to fit in with such false teachers as Peter Ruckman, and Gail Riplinger.

I suggest you remove these words when talking about our King James Bible or any other translation of the Bible. All of these above five terms rightly **belong only** to the Hebrew, Aramaic, and Greek Words that God Himself spoke. These five terms **do not belong** to those words that man translated into the languages of the world. If you want to discuss this further, you can call me at **856-854-4747** and I would be glad to talk with you about it.

Ruckman's & Riplinger's Positions

QUESTION #931

Since Dr. Hymers had written a book on Ruckman, *Ruckmanism Exposed*, I figured I'd ask him if he had any insight on the question whether or not Ruckman goes as far as Riplinger in regards to inspired Bibles in all languages. What do you think about this?

ANSWER #931

I believe that Peter Ruckman is in agreement with Gail Riplinger in all of these matters that you mentioned. Neither of them should be followed by any Bible-believing Christians. They both believe you don't any longer need God's own Hebrew, Aramaic, and Greek Words that He gave us and preserved for us in the Words underlying the King James Bible. They wrongly and heretically believe that the King James Bible was inspired by God and therefore supplants and replaces God's own Hebrew, Aramaic, and Greek Words.

Preservation of Original Words

QUESTION #932

I am listening to Dr. Waite's audio response to Gail Riplinger's *Traitors'* booklet. One thing that he has said over and over again is that the King James Bible is not "*given by inspiration*" (which I agree with), but that the Hebrew, Aramaic, and Greek Words underlying the King James Bible were the Words originally given by God by inspiration and which have been preserved. What is not clear from the audio (thus far) is (1) Do we still have these texts today? (I assume we do and that God has continued to preserve His Word in the original languages), and (2) What are they called, if I should wish to get a hold of them? Is Scrivener's Greek Textus Receptus the correct Greek text to use for the New Testament? And what should be used for the Old Testament?

ANSWER #932

I believe *Scrivener's Annotated Greek New Testament* has the preserved Greek Words of the originals for today. We have it as **BFT #1670 @ $35 + $8.00 S&H**. This is a large print copy of Scrivener's original book with all the features included. I believe God has preserved the original Hebrew and Aramaic Old Testament Words have been preserved for us also. We have those Words in a Hebrew/King James Bible parallel edition. It is **BFT #2064 @ $90.00 + $8.00 S&H**. It keeps going up in price, but this is what it is presently.

QUESTION #933

I have just listened to your audio files answering Gail Riplinger. It answers quite a few questions I had in my mind about her position regarding the King James Bible. It's tragic to think you have to spend so much time dealing with her many mistakes, and her personal attacks on you and others. I'm horrified to think Gail called your *Defined King James Bible* the "*Defiled Bible*." For a King James lover to say such a thing proves she is truly outside God's will in pursuing her personal crusade. From this distance, to say that even sounds blasphemous. I will remove the link with "*AV publications*" off my blogsite forthwith! Will she stop her attacks? Will you answer her attacks?

ANSWER #933

Thank you for your insightful comments on the Gail Riplinger situation. You have put your criticisms of Gail Riplinger in proper terms. In answer to your questions, I do not believe she will stop her attacks. They are continuing even as I write this. Will I answer her attacks? Perhaps some of them, depending on what they are and how many there are in the future. It may very well be that it is a waste of time. I have already answered some of these attacks. The many documents that are in print that have answered her lies might very well be almost sufficient in this department of truth.

Riplinger And My KJB Views

QUESTION #934

I haven't been much in contact with you in recent times, but you have not been entirely out of mind. I was sorry to notice from the Dean Burgon Society website some huge controversy going on, over Gail Riplinger's love life! That must be giving you huge "grief." I wonder how the outcome of your correspondence with the lady affects the standing of the King James Bible?

ANSWER #934

Riplinger's false and heretical view of the King James Bible does not affect my Biblical view of the KJB. For me, it is an accurate, faithful and sound translation, not a direct, inspired revelation from God as she wrongly teaches. Time will tell about how the battle with Gail Riplinger turns out in the future years with all of her lies and twisting of truth. I believe we will be victorious over her many falsifications by showing forth the truth. She is a woman who is completely out of place by "*teaching*" and "*usurping authority over*" men in the areas of theology and Bible doctrine. In many ways, Gail Riplinger is a modern-day Jezebel.

1 Timothy 2:12 *"But I suffer **not a woman to teach, nor to usurp authority over the man**, but to be in silence."*

CHAPTER XII
QUESTIONS ABOUT
WOMEN PREACHERS

Should Women Teach Men?

QUESTION #935

Are women preachers Biblical? Should women teach men?

ANSWER #935

Women preachers are not Biblical. Nor is it Biblical for women to teach men only, or even to teach a class that has both women and men together in it. I am working on 1 Timothy to publish as our next *PREACHING VERSE BY VERSE* book. I just went over this theme the other day in my first draft. Here is what I have written on it.

[As of this date, the book has now been published and can be obtained from the Bible For Today as **BFT #3085 @ $15.00 + $4.00 S&H.**]

1 Timothy 2:12 *"But I suffer **not a woman to teach, nor to usurp authority over the man**, but to be in silence."*

The word for *"suffer"* is EPITREPO. It means: *"to turn to, transfer, commit, instruct; to permit, allow, give leave."* In other words, God does not permit or allow *"a woman to teach, nor to usurp authority over the man."* According to the Words of God, there should be no women preachers of any kind. Yet, as of 1989, here are some of the numbers of women in full-time church ministry:

4,743 in the United Methodist churches

4,000 in the Assemblies of God churches

2,419 in the Presbyterian Church U.S.A. churches

1,803 in the United Church of Christ churches

1,358 in the Evangelical Lutheran churches

1,225 in the Southern Baptist churches

This totals 155,480 in *"full-time church ministry."* 84 of the 166 denominations in our country ordain women to full-time ministry. In 1989, this was 7.9% of all the U.S. clergy (*National & International Religion Report*, March 13, 1989).

In a more current study, the following was found:

*"U. S. Federal labor statistics indicate that the number of women who describe themselves as 'clergy' increased from **16,408 in 1983** to **43,542 in 1996**. As of 1996, 1 in ever 8 clergy is female in the U.S. The percentage of female graduate students at 229 North American Christian schools of theology has risen from **10% in 1972** to **30% in 1997**. In some schools of theology, over 50% of the students are women."*

The Scriptures are clear about women preachers. The word used for *"usurp authority"* is AUTHENTEO. It means various things:

*"one who with his own hands kills another or himself; **one who acts on his own authority, autocratic; an absolute master; to govern, exercise dominion over one**."*

In other words, a *"woman"* is not allowed by God to *"exercise dominion"* or be an *"absolute master"* over the *"man"* (which is ARSEN or *"male"*). The Women's Liberation Movement does not go along with this verse at all.

The Lord Jesus Christ has the proper *"authority."* There are many uses of *"authority"* in the New Testament. Here are a few examples:

Matthew 7:29 *"For he taught them as one having **authority**, and not as the scribes."*

John 5:27 *"And hath given him **authority** to execute judgment also, because he is the Son of man."*

Acts 9:14 *"And here he hath **authority** from the chief priests to bind all that call on thy name."*

Titus 2:15 *"These things speak, and exhort, and rebuke with all **authority**. Let no man despise thee."*

When I was a student at Dallas Theological Seminary, I worked at a Baptist Mexican Mission for a year or so. A woman was my superior in that mission. After a while, I had to resign because When I became the pastor, the woman didn't find herself "under" me, but continued to "manage" me in the affairs of that mission church.

The first church I pastored after my five years on active duty as a Naval Chaplain was Immanuel Baptist Church in Newton, Massachusetts. One of the most outspoken women in the congregation was the wife of a powerful deacon. It was said that she made the "snowballs," but he threw them. She was a woman out of place. I remember one particular night I was trying to turn the lights in the church off. She did not want those lights turned off so there was a battle over the light switch. It was a mess.

In summary, as I said before, I do not believe women should teach either men's classes, or mixed classes of men and women in Sunday School or in other situations. I firmly believe that this practice is contrary to this verse.

There is no Biblical prohibition for women to teach women, but men should teach men and mixed classes of men and women.

Why Women Preachers?

QUESTION #936

There seems to be many women preachers in our country and in other countries around the world. Why do you think women become preachers?

ANSWER #936

I'm sure the answer would vary from one woman to another. Perhaps it is because there is a lack of men who enter the ministry. This is often the excuse as to why single women enter the mission field. They say it is because there are so few men who want to go. In any event, those women who enter the ministry must do so because they do not find anything in the Bible that would convince them that this is unscriptural. In addition to that, there is a lack of conviction on the part of theological schools and seminaries that women preachers are unscriptural. Because of this lack of conviction, these institutions are willing to train women for becoming ministers. The schools must bear some the blame as well as the women who enter the ministry. Without the schools to train them, they would not be able to become women preachers.

CHAPTER XIII
QUESTIONS ABOUT THE
BIBLE'S INSPIRATION

QUESTION #937

Why is it heretical to think that the King James Bible (or any translation) is "*inspired*"?

ANSWER #937

Though our King James Bible is the only true, faithful, and accurate English translation of the proper and preserved Hebrew, Aramaic, and Greek Words, there is not a verse of the Bible that speaks it (or any other **translation** of the Words of God) as being either "*given by inspiration of God,*" "*God-breathed,*" "*inspired of God,*" "*verbally inspired,*" or "***inspired***" in any sense of that word, including "*derivative inspiration,*" "*indirect inspiration,*" "*having the mark of inspiration,*" "*inspired in a 'generic' or general sense*" or any other similar terms that might be brought up to modify "*inspired*" or "*inspiration.*"

2 Timothy 3:16-17 deals with how God gave us His Words in Hebrew, Aramaic, and Greek. The use of the words, "*inspired*" or "*inspiration*" for "**translations**" is man-made. It is a serious misuse of either of these terms. Once you use either of these terms for "**translations**," who is to say that they cannot be applied, not only to the King James Bible, but also to the NIV, NASV, NKJV, ESV, RSV, NRSV, and all the English translations as well as the hundreds of other language translations around the world? Where can you draw the line? Where is any proof that they are or are not "*inspired,*" once you assume that the term, "*inspiration,*" can be properly applied to "**translations**"?

One of the proofs that God did not "*inspire*" the Authorized Version of 1611 is that it contained the Apocrypha. The Apocrypha is filled with errors and contradictions against the true Bible. If indeed God breathed-out, or "*inspired*" the King James Bible, our God would be guilty of error and sin. It would be calling God a liar. That is unthinkable. Then, if you say the King James Bible is "*inspired*" (or use any of these terms listed above), which edition of the King James Bible is it that is "*inspired*"? Is it edition #1, #2, #3,

#4, #5, #6, or #7? Then, even if it is the 7th edition, which publisher's edition #7 is it? That published by Moody, Zondervan, Cambridge, Oxford, etc? There are many differences in these editions. If it was actually *"given by inspiration of God,"* why are there so many changes in it through the years?

God's *"inspired"* Words are limited to His own Words which are exclusively Hebrew, a little Aramaic, and Greek. The King James Bible is the only accurate, faithful, and true English translation of those Words, but it should not and cannot be called *"given by inspiration of God," "God-breathed," "inspired of God," "verbally inspired,"* or *"**inspired**"* in any sense of that word, including *"derivative inspiration," "indirect inspiration," "having the mark of inspiration," "inspired in a 'generic' or general sense"* or any other similar terms that might be brought up to modify *"inspired"* or *"inspiration."*

QUESTION #938

Charles-Carlo-Buzzetti, wrote: *"God **inspired prophets**, evangelists, scholars, and apostles to write their **messages** in the human form."* Is this man right?

ANSWER #938

This man is in error in two ways: (1) the *"prophets"* were not *"inspired"* or *"breathed-out by God."* It is the **Words** that God *"inspired"* and *"breathed-out."* God did not *"breathe-out"* the *"prophets."* The prophets were *"moved"* by God the Holy Spirit (2 Peter 1:21). (2) It was not merely the *"messages,"* but the very Hebrew, Aramaic, and Greek **"Words"** that God gave to His prophets that were *"breathed-out"* and *"inspired by God."*

Which "Inspired" Hebrew & Greek
QUESTION #939

I was reading on your website that you do not believe the King James Bible is *"inspired."* You believe that only the Hebrew, Aramaic, and Greek original Words are the *"inspired Words of God."* I would like for someone to answer these few questions of mine as clearly as possible.

1. Which Words (OT and NT) are *"inspired,"* seeing as there are several compilations of each that are not compatible with each other.
2. Why are only these Words *"inspired"*?
3. Is it the texts or the Words that are *"inspired of God"*?
4. How is it that these Words were *"inspired,"* yet, according to you, nothing else is?

These are questions that have plagued me for several months concerning the English version issue.

ANSWER #939

1. I believe the *"Traditional"* Hebrew, Aramaic, and Greek Words are *"inspired."* Since there are a few of those *"Traditional"* Words which have slight differences, my personal conviction, after studying this subject since 1972, is that the *"Traditional"* Hebrew, Aramaic and Greek Words that underlie the King James Bible are the ones which were *"given by inspiration of God"* and *"God-breathed"* and have been preserved for us.

2. Because 2 Timothy 3:16 teaches that THEOPNEUSTOS (*"God-breathed"*) Words were the Ones He *"breathed out"* originally. Since I believe the Hebrew, Aramaic, and Greek Words underlying the King James Bible are the preserved copies of those original Words, I believe the THEOPNEUSTOS (*"God-breathed"*) Words are those and those alone.

3. It is the exact **Words** which are THEOPNEUSTOS (*"God-breathed"*), not the *"texts."*

4. Because, as I have stated in your question #2 above, 2 Timothy 3:16 teaches that only the THEOPNEUSTOS (*"God-breathed"*) Words were the Ones He *"breathed out"* originally. He has not duplicated His *"inspired"* Words in any other fashion. These are the *"Words"* that should be accurately translated in all the languages of the world.

Doctrinal Statement Confusion
QUESTION #940

Is the following statement true as far as you are concerned? I am not asking is this the same wording, etc., as your church's statement of faith. I am asking is it biblically correct? If not why?

> *"We believe the* **Bible** *to be the written revelation of God, complete and sufficient in all respects. We believe the* **Scriptures** *to be* **"God-breathed"** *and therefore fully authoritative in and of themselves; they rely for their authority upon no church, council, or creed, but are authoritative simply because they are the Word of God. The* **Scriptures**, *as they embody the very speaking of God, partake of His authority, His power."*

ANSWER #940

Here is a statement I would make regarding the *"**Bible**."* It is clear as to which *"**Bible**"* I am talking about without any question:

> *"It is my own personal conviction and belief, after studying this subject since 1971, that the Words of the Received*

Greek and Masoretic Hebrew texts that underlie the King James Bible are the very Words which God has preserved down through the centuries, being the exact Words of the originals themselves. As such, I believe they are inspired Words. I believe they are preserved Words. I believe they are inerrant Words. I believe they are infallible Words. This is why I believe so strongly that any valid translation must be based upon these original language texts, and these alone!"

The statement that you quoted above is very ambiguous because it does not define what is meant by either the word, "**Bible**," or the word, "**Scriptures**," you are speaking about that are "**God-breathed**"? Is this statement referring to the Hebrew, Aramaic, and Greek Words underlying the King James Bible which are "**God-breathed**"? Or are you referring to the King James Bible words which are **not** "**God-breathed**" or words of some other translation which are **not** "**God-breathed**"? This is very confusing and unclear. It should be revised carefully and clearly.

CHAPTER XIV
QUESTIONS ABOUT 22
MISCELLANEOUS TOPICS

1. Questions About The Trinity

1 John 5:7-8

QUESTION #941

1 John 5:7 *"For there are Three that bear record [__in heaven, the Father, the Word and the Holy Ghost: and these three are one.__"*
1 John 5:8 *"__And there are three that bear witness in earth,__] the Spirit, and the water, and the blood: and these three agree in one."*

I have a question I hope you can answer. I am a firm believer in the King James Bible as the preserved Word of God in English. My pastor said that the last part *"and these three are one"* was never written and cannot be found in any of the transcripts of old. I have a Scofield Bible and it even says that the complete verse is *"generally agreed that v. 7 has no real authority, and has been inserted."* This came about during a study of the idea of the "Trinity" and this is the only clear verse that says it. This is troublesome as if it was inserted, how many more were inserted?

ANSWER #941

As to your question on 1 John 5:7-8, let me say this. No doubt your pastor believes in the Gnostic Critical Greek Text as did the Old Scofield Bible editors. There are three things I would like to comment on:

(1) There are more words than just *"and these three are one"* that are omitted in the Gnostic Critical Greek Text. All the words that are **bold and underlined** in the verses above are omitted by that false Greek Text.

(2) It is not true to say that this passage about the Trinity and that *"this is the only clear verse that says it."* While this section teaches there is a Trinity, the Trinity is also found clearly in other verses.

Matthew 28:19: *"Go ye therefore, and teach all nations, baptizing them in the name of the **Father**, and of the **Son**, and of the **Holy Ghost**:"*

Matthew 3:16-17: *"And **Jesus**, when he was baptized, went up straightway out of the water: and, lo, the heavens were opened unto him, and he saw the **Spirit of God** descending like a dove, and lighting upon him: And lo **a voice from heaven**, saying, This is my beloved Son, in whom I am well pleased."*

Mark 1:9-11: *"And it came to pass in those days, that **Jesus** came from Nazareth of Galilee, and was baptized of John in Jordan. And straightway coming up out of the water, he saw the heavens opened, and **the Spirit** like a dove descending upon him: And there came **a voice from heaven**, saying, Thou art my beloved Son, in whom I am well pleased."*

Luke 3:21-22: *"Now when all the people were baptized, it came to pass, that **Jesus** also being baptized, and praying, the heaven was opened, And the **Holy Ghost** descended in a bodily shape like a dove upon him, and **a voice came from heaven**, which said, Thou art my beloved Son; in thee I am well pleased."*

Galatians 4:4 *"But when the fulness of the time was come, **God** sent forth his **Son**, made of a woman, made under the law, To redeem them that were under the law, that we might receive the adoption of sons. And because ye are sons, **God** hath sent forth the **Spirit** of his **Son** into your hearts, crying, Abba, **Father**."*

John 16:12-15 *"**I** have yet many things to say unto you, but ye cannot bear them now. Howbeit when he, the **Spirit** of truth, is come, he will guide you into all truth: for he shall not speak of himself; but whatsoever he shall hear, that shall he speak: and he will shew you things to come. He shall glorify **me**: for he shall receive of **mine**, and shall shew it unto you. All things that the **Father** hath are **mine**: therefore said I, that he shall take of **mine**, and shall shew it unto you."*

John 15:26 *"But when the **Comforter** is come, whom I will send unto you from the **Father**, even the **Spirit** of truth, which proceedeth from the **Father**, he shall testify of **me**:"*

These are a few of the verses in the New Testament that teach clearly, in addition to 1 John 5:7-8, that our God is a Trinity with three Persons, God the Father, God the Son, and God the Holy Spirit.

(3) 1 John 5:7-8 were not "*inserted*" as your pastor has stated. They were in the original writing of the verses. For abundant evidence of the authenticity in the manuscripts for 1 John 5:7-8, I suggest that you go to page 299 of Dr. Jack Moorman's book, *Early Manuscripts, Church Fathers and the Authorized Version* (**BFT #3230** @ **$20.00** + **$7.00 S&H**). You can order this with your credit card at **856-854-4452** if you wish.

2. Questions About Marriage One Man and One Woman

QUESTION #942

I am currently living and working in Monrovia, Liberia. This topic has come up from time to time. I would like your opinion of any Scriptures which actually **forbid a man from having more then one wife**. Most arguments that I have seen are based on "types," "pictures," and the like. I would love to have something from Scripture that is clearly against it.

ANSWER #942

I will give you a few Scriptures that teach that a man should have only one living wife. The pastor/bishop/elder of a local church must be the "*husband of one wife*" (1 Timothy 3:2; Titus 1:6). The deacons must also be the "*husband of one wife*" (1 Timothy 3:12).

When God created man and woman, He provided only one man and one wife. Ephesians 5:31 states: "*For this cause shall a man leave his father and mother, and shall be joined unto his wife, and they two shall be one flesh.*"

Here is only one "MAN" and one "WIFE." There are no New Testament sanctions for multiple wives, though it was practiced in the Old Testament. Matthew 19:5 "*And said, For this cause shall a **man** leave father and mother, and shall cleave to his **wife**: and they twain shall be one flesh?*"

Here again it is one man and only one wife here.

Polygamy is being pushed in our country now. It is sad that President Barack Obama nominated for commissioner of the Equal Employment Opportunity Commission (EEOC) a woman who signed a radical manifesto **endorsing polygamy**. I thought our nation had settled the polygamy issue a century and a half ago, but this nomination makes it a 21st century controversy. Obama's nominee for the EEOC is a lesbian law-school professor named Chai R. Feldblum. She signed a 2006 manifesto **endorsing**

polygamous households (i.e., "*in which there is more than one conjugal partner*"). [http://www.beyondmarriage.org/signatories.html]

Feldblum is not the only **pro-polygamy** Obama appointee. His Regulatory Czar, Cass Sunstein, wrote a book in 2008 called *Nudge: Improving Decisions About Health, Wealth and Happiness* in which he urged that "*the word marriage would no longer appear in any laws, and marriage licenses would no longer be offered or recognized by any level of government.*" http://www.wnd.com/index.php?pageId=113802

The Defense of Marriage Act (DOMA) was passed in 1996 [http://www.eagleforum.org/topics/marriage/] by overwhelming majorities in Congress and signed by President Bill Clinton. The Government Accountability Office (GAO) has identified more than 1,000 federal laws that are based on the **traditional definition of marriage**, including the tax laws that permit married couples the advantage of filing joint income tax returns and the Social Security benefits awarded to full-time homemakers, both very popular federal laws.

The peculiar push to **recognize polygamy** as just another variety of marriage is a predictable and logical corollary of the political movement to recognize same-sex marriage. If our government cannot define marriage as the union of one man and one woman, it follows that there can be no law against the union of a man and several women.

For years, **polygamy**, even though it is totally demeaning to women, has been embraced by the powerful American Civil Liberties Union (ACLU). Polygamy is one of the many controversial issues that were not raised during ACLU lawyer Ruth Bader Ginsburg's so-friendly Supreme Court confirmation hearings.

The ACLU's feminist president, Nadine Strossen, stated in a speech [http://www.wnd.com/news/article.asp?ARTICLE_ID=44977] at Yale University in June 2005 that the ACLU defends "*the right of individuals to engage in polygamy.*" On October 15, 2006, in a high-profile debate against Supreme Court Justice Antonin Scalia, Strossen stated that the **ACLU supports the right to polygamy**.

Speaking to the Federalist Society on November 18, 2006, the ACLU's executive director, Anthony Romero, confirmed his organization's **support of polygamy**. [http://capwiz.com/eagleforum/utr/1/EXXHLOYCRU/JBJPLOYDAB/4224184116]

The massive immigration that the United States has accepted in recent years includes large numbers of **immigrants from Third World countries that approve of polygamy** as well as marriage to children and to close relatives. We wonder if **polygamists** have been admitted to the U.S. and if they are continuing these customs in U.S. neighborhoods.

Attacks on the traditional legal definition of marriage come from the gay lobby seeking social recognition of their lifestyle, from the anti-marriage feminists, and from some libertarians who believe marriage should be merely a private affair, none of the government's business. These libertarians want to deny government the right to define marriage, set its standards, or issue marriage licenses.

Government now has and should have a very important role in defining who may get a license to marry. **In America, it is and should be a criminal offense to marry more than one person at a time, or marry a child or a close relative, even though such practices are common in some foreign countries.**

In Socialist Canada, which has already approved same-sex marriage, **polygamy has suddenly become a live issue.** British Columbia's Supreme Court is now being asked to decide if **polygamy** should remain illegal.

3. Questions Pertaining To The U. S. Constitution

E-Mails And the Constitution
QUESTION #943

I made some strong objections to what you had written in one of your e-mails against the practices of President Obama and those in his administration. I asked to be dropped from your mailing list. After my letter I have not received any more e-mails from the Bible For Today. Why is this? I ask you to reinstate my E-mail as someone who is supportive of BFT and your gospel ministry and messages, so that I may receive timely E-mails from you (just not ones which are politically charged).

ANSWER #943

Our **Bible For Today** has but one E-mail list. You asked to be dropped from it, so you have received nothing of any kind after your request to be dropped. If you don't like my strong defense of the U. S. Constitutional government and my strong exposure of anything or anyone (including our President, our Congress, or our courts) who oppose U. S. Constitutional government, you have only to push the delete button. The only way you can receive our materials is to request to be put back on to our E-mail list. Once you request to be reinstated on our e-mail list, we will honor your request just as we honored your request to be dropped. But you must understand that we cannot be selective in sending you our Bible For Today materials. The way our e-mail system is set up, you must receive **all** of them, or **none** of them.

Forced Union Dues
QUESTION #944
Why do I have to pay dues to the union where I work? Not only are they forcing me to pay the dues, but if I appeal the payment of the dues, the union has to approve the place where the dues money will go. They made it clear that this money cannot go to any religious organization such as my church.

ANSWER #944
It is all completely contrary to our United States Constitution. It sounds like your company has voted for a "*closed union shop.*" I suppose they would oppose the sending of your dues to any conservative group you might want to send them to. They would only sanction far-left groups. They have already prohibited giving to your church. It sounds like stealing to me. "*Thou shalt not steal.*" I'm sorry for your situation.

Non-Union Paying Union Dues
QUESTION #945
I am being forced to pay my "*fair share*" of union dues because the union in my school in which I work has voted to make us non-union workers pay. We had no say in the vote. I have contacted the CLA and the National Right to Work Legal Defense Foundation. I now know what I need to do; however, I need some help because of the short time that I have to protest. Do you have some Bible verses that question whether there should be unions?

ANSWER #945
Here are a few Bible verses that teach to me that "*servants*" or employees today should do as their "*masters*" or employers require. If the verses were applied for today, there would be no unions that fight with their employers. If a worker doesn't like his work, let him or her quit work and work for someone else.

I worked for 19 years in the School District of Philadelphia as a non-union teacher. I was never made to pay union dues. I'm sorry that you have been made to pay dues when you are a non-member. It is unconstitutional and wrong.

> "**_Servants, be obedient to them that are your masters_**
> *according to the flesh, with fear and trembling, in singleness of your heart, as unto Christ; 6 Not with eyeservice, as menpleasers; but **as the servants of Christ**, doing the will of God from the heart; 7 With good will*

doing service, as to the Lord, and not to men: 8 Knowing that whatsoever good thing any man doeth, the same shall he receive of the Lord, whether he be bond or free." (Ephesians 6:5-8)

"Servants, obey in all things your masters according to the flesh; not with eyeservice, as menpleasers; but in singleness of heart, fearing God:" (Colossians 3:22)

"Let as many servants as are under the yoke count their own masters worthy of all honour, that the name of God and his doctrine be not blasphemed." (1 Timothy 6:1)

"Exhort servants to be obedient unto their own masters, and to please them well in all things; not answering again;" (Titus 2:9)

"Servants, be subject to your masters with all fear; not only to the good and gentle, but also to the froward." (1 Peter 2:18)

Payment For Gun Ownership
QUESTION #946

Is it true that Senate Bill SB-2099 will require owners of firearms to pay a $50 charge per gun and to list each gun they own on their federal tax form?

ANSWER #946

The answer is "No." This Internet rumor states that SB-2099 is legislation currently being considered by the Senate. The bill supposedly requires owners of firearms to list on their 1040 tax return all guns they own and then pay a $50 charge per firearm. There is no such legislation by this name in the 111th Congress.

This is a false rumor. Snopes can't be trusted. Not only do I go to truthorfiction.com to check out rumors, but I go to the source listed. This time, I went to www.senate.gov and typed in the SB 2099 number and checked it out as well.

4. Questions About
the Spanish Bible
Received Text Spanish Bible
QUESTION #947

I attend a Bible Church. I greatly appreciate your ministry. In the past, I have ordered several of your books and Bibles. I have a question that I hope you can answer. A teenage girl at my church wants to learn Spanish. She is interested in a Bible that has the King James Version as well as a Spanish version of the Bible. However, I'm aware that Spanish Bible versions may be based either on the critical text or on the received text. Do you know any Spanish Bible versions which are accurate and based on the received text?

ANSWER #947

The Reina/Valera/Gomez (RVG) Spanish Bible is faithful both to the Textus Receptus and to the King James Bible. Dr. Gomez also has published a parallel version with the Spanish RVG on one side and the King James Bible on the other side. If you want to get a copy, with your credit card, you can call and order it at **856-854-4452** if you wish.

My Knowledge of Spanish

QUESTION #948

I would like to know Dr. D. A. Waite's personal knowledge of the Spanish Language? Where did he study Spanish? Can you help me? This will determine our use of the Reina Valera Gomez for our congregation.

ANSWER #948

I learned my Spanish as follows: (1) two years in High School; (2) two years at the University of Michigan, (3) having a man from Chile as a roommate at the University of Michigan, conversing with him and his friends in Spanish daily, (4) preaching for two years in Spanish to Mexicans in Dallas, Texas who didn't know English, (5) using Spanish with those from Latin American countries while teaching English for 19 years in the School District of Philadelphia. The Reina Valera Gomez is the most accurate Spanish translation in print today. I recommend its use for you and your congregation.

5. Questions About Christ's Bodily Resurrection

The Day of the Crucifixion

QUESTION #949

Was Jesus crucified on Friday? Some say He was crucified on Wednesday or Thursday? On what day was Jesus crucified?

ANSWER #949

I believe the answer to this question hinges on the following two verses, one from the Old Testament, and one from the New Testament:

Jonah 1:17 *"Now the LORD had prepared a great fish to swallow up Jonah. And Jonah was in the belly of the fish **three days and three nights**."*

Matthew 12:40 *"For as Jonas was **three days and three nights in the whale's belly**; so shall the Son of man be **three days and three nights in the heart of the earth**."*

In the first place, all Bible interpretations should agree that Matthew 12:40 refers to the predictions by the Lord Jesus Christ of exactly how long He would be buried in Joseph of Arimathaea's tomb. It had to be exactly as long as Jonah was *"in the belly of the fish,"* that is exactly *"**three days and three nights**"* (Jonah 1:17). If this was true, let's reconstruct the events spoken of in Matthew 27:57-60:

*"**When the even was come**,* [after 6:00 p.m. Wednesday, Jewish time] *there came a rich man of Arimathaea, named Joseph, who also himself was Jesus' disciple: He went to Pilate, and **begged the body of Jesus**. Then Pilate commanded the body to be delivered. And **when Joseph had taken the body**, he wrapped it in a clean linen cloth, And **laid it in his own new tomb**, which he had hewn out in the rock: and he rolled a great stone to the door of the sepulchre, and departed."* (Matthew 27:57-60)

I believe that these *"**three days and three nights**"* are to interpreted very literally as 72 hours. If the Lord Jesus Christ were crucified and buried on Friday, as tradition wrongly assumes, it would be impossible for Him to be in the tomb for 72 hours. Only if *"days"* could be interpreted as part of a day and only if the three *"nights"* would be totally erased, could a Friday crucifixion and a Sunday bodily resurrection be possible.

The Bible's definition of a solar *"day"* in Genesis chapter 1 is the *"**the evening and the morning**"* for each of the six days of God's creation of the world.

Genesis 1:5 *And God called the light Day, and the darkness he called Night. And **the evening and the morning were the first day**.*

Genesis 1:8 *And God called the firmament Heaven. And **the evening and the morning were the second day**.*

Genesis 1:13 *And **the evening and the morning were the third day**.*

Genesis 1:19 *And **the evening and the morning were the fourth day**.*

Genesis 1:23 *And **the evening and the morning were the fifth day**.*

Genesis 1:31 *And God saw every thing that he had made, and, behold, it was very good. And **the evening and the morning were***

the sixth day.

Notice when the bodily resurrection of the Lord Jesus Christ took place according to each of the four Gospels:

> **Matthew 28:1** *"In the end of the sabbath, as it began to dawn toward **the first day of the week**, came Mary Magdalene and the other Mary to see the sepulchre."*
>
> **Mark 16:2** *"And very early in the morning **the first day of the week**, they came unto the sepulchre at the rising of the sun."*
>
> **Luke 24:1** *"Now upon **the first day of the week**, very early in the morning, they came unto the sepulchre, bringing the spices which they had prepared, and certain others with them."*
>
> **John 20:1** *"**The first day of the week** cometh Mary Magdalene early, when it was yet dark, unto the sepulchre, and seeth the stone taken away from the sepulchre."*

> If indeed the bodily resurrection of the Lord Jesus Christ took place, as all four Gospels tell us, on *"**the first day of the week**"* (the Jewish *"Sunday"*), it had to be some time after 6:00 p.m.--our *"Saturday"* night which is the Jewish *"Sunday"* morning, since Jewish days began after 6:00 p.m. the day before. Since there had to be literally 72 hours for the Lord Jesus Christ to be in the tomb, He would have to have been crucified on Wednesday, and placed in that tomb on Wednesday at or slightly after 6:00 p.m. which would have been the beginning of the Jewish Thursday. He would then have been the tomb Thursday day and Thursday night, Friday day and Friday night, and Saturday day and Saturday night. His resurrection would be at or slightly after 6:00 p.m.--our Saturday night which was the Jewish Sunday morning, at the beginning of that day. That timing would alone fulfill the requirement of the Lord Jesus Christ's body to be *"**three days and three nights in the heart of the earth**."*

That is what I, and many other Bible teachers, believe about the day of the Lord Jesus Christ's crucifixion, burial, and bodily resurrection in literal fulfillment of the 72 hours required by His Words recorded in Matthew 12:40 as He quoted from Jonah 1:17.

6. Questions About The *Defined King James Bible*

Defined King James Bible Editions

QUESTION #950

Thanks for your quick shipment of your *Defined King James Bible*. Please tell me if there are any differences between 10th and 9th editions.

ANSWER #950

The 10th printing of the *Defined King James Bible* is called the "*Third Revised Edition.*" The differences are explained in p. xxxi of that "*Third Revised Edition.*" I made changes on over 82 pages of this edition by changing references to the Hebrew, Aramaic, and Greek from only the "<u>Word</u>" of God to the "<u>Words</u>" of God. As explained on page xxxi, at least six fundamentalist schools that are listed (led by Bob Jones University) in their written and spoken materials deny the Bible Preservation of the "<u>Words</u>" of God, but believe only in the Bible Preservation of the "<u>Word</u>" of God. They define "<u>Word</u>" of God as only the "*message, thoughts, ideas, concepts, truth, doctrine, or revelation*" of God, but not the preservation of the original Hebrew, Aramaic, and Greek "<u>Words</u>" of God. That's what the believe about Bible preservation. A very defective view which is not preservation at all.

1611 King James Bible

QUESTION #951

I ordered two of the *Defined King James Bibles* from your website, but it does not appear to be the "1611" King James Bible, which is what I wanted. Please confirm.

ANSWER #951

Our *Defined King James Bible* is the current 1769 edition of the 1611 King James Bible. <u>If you mean the original wording and spelling, this is the 1st edition.</u> The present cost is about **$45.00 + $8.00 S&H**. If you want that instead of the one you have, you could return your order and pay the difference in costs. You can call us at **856-854-4452** if you wish to ask further questions on this.

Why the Diamonds in the DKJB
QUESTION #952
While reading *The Defined King James Bible*, I often find a diamond shaped symbol at the end of some verses. However, I cannot find why it is there. An example is Hebrews 12:29. Could you tell me why you put a diamond there? Also if there is a page number explaining it, where would it be?

ANSWER #952
These little diamonds mark the 85-verse daily Bible reading sections. They are explained in the *Defined King James Bible* at the top of pages viii and ix.

The 4,114 DKJB Definitions Book
QUESTION #953
I have two more questions. How many pages are in the *4,114 Definitions* book which were taken from the *Defined King James Bible*? Also, what are the dimensions of that book? I'm just trying to figure out if it's small enough to fit in my Bible case.

ANSWER #953
The dimensions of that booklet are the same as those of the Defined King James Bible. The size is 5.5" x 8.5."

Unbound DKJB Bibles
QUESTION #954
Is it possible to purchase a medium-size print *Defined King James Bible* that is unbound, and printed on large size print Bible paper? If not able to print on large print paper, can one purchase one of these Bibles that is unbound?

ANSWER #954
At the present time, we have only bound copies of our *Defined King James Bibles*.

DKJB & Hymn Book Purchase
QUESTION #955
My wife and I have recently been listening to your services and finding them to be edifying. I'm inquiring on purchasing a hymn book but do not see it available on your website. May I purchase one of these? I've also been told that your *Defined King James Bible* is a must! Would you have this in large print? I noticed that it says medium print. I'm not familiar with this. Is this

comparable to large print? Praise God for the ministry that your church does. May He bless you richly.

ANSWER #955

I am very pleased that you have been attending our services here at the **Bible For Today Baptist Church** in Collingswood, New Jersey and have found them to be edifying. We welcome you to our ministry. If you also listen to our Bible Discussion studies at 1:30 p.m. Sunday, please call my cell phone (**856-261-9018**) and say hello to the folks here, or you can also send an e-mail to questions@bftbc.org and we can welcome you officially. If you listen to our Bible Study discussion and prayer service Thursdays from 8:00 p.m. to 9:15 p.m. (Eastern), you can call in and/or email us as well. We welcome comments and questions during these two services.

As to our hymn book, I would be glad to have the publisher drop ship a copy directly to your address if you give it to me.

As to our *Defined King James Bible*, we have them in medium print (10-point type) at about 6" x 8" size. We also have them in large print (12-point type (at about 9" x 11" size. The medium is **$35.00 + $7.00 S&H** for genuine leather (the hardback is **$15.00 + $7.00 S&H**). The large is **$40.00 + $7.00 S&H** for genuine leather (the hardback is **$20.00 + $7.00 S&H**). They come in black or burgundy colors. If you have a credit card, you could call in the number at either **856-854-4452** or at my direct line phone **856-854-4747** and I would see to it that your order would go out, both for the hymn book and for the Bible. Please give us your complete address when you order so we can send these things to you. Again, welcome to our church ministry as we continue to *"preach the Word"* (2 Timothy 4:2) on a verse-by-verse basis from the King James Bible. I'll be waiting to hear from you.

7. Questions About
The Lord's Supper
My Body and My Blood
QUESTION #956

I am a Lutheran pastor in Ohio. There are some of the *Defined King James Bibles* in our pews. But, I wonder, as a Baptist pastor how you look at three passages concerning the Lord's Supper.

1. 1 Corinthians 11:24 and Matthew 26:28:
    *"And when he had given thanks, he brake it, and said, Take, eat: **this is my body**, which is broken for you: this do in remembrance of me."*
    Matthew 26:28 *"For **this is my blood** of the new testament,*

which is shed for many for the remission of sins."

It seems to me, as a Lutheran theologian that when the Lord Jesus said, *"this is My body,"* and *"this is My blood,"* here in 1 Corinthians 10:16 and Matthew 26:28, the Apostle Paul would indicate that somehow the Lord is giving us His body and His blood in His Supper.

2.   1 Corinthians 11:29:

> *"For **he that eateth and drinketh unworthily**, eateth and drinketh damnation to himself, **not discerning the Lord's body**."*

In the words, *"he that eateth and drinketh unworithily . . . not discerning the body,"* it seems that the Apostle is again indicating that more than just the bread and the cup is involved. In fact, it seems that it is a serious warning and circumstance. I ask about these two passages, not to debate, but rather to find out how you would look at these two passages in particular and what they are teaching.

ANSWER #956

Let me briefly give my opinion on the two parts of your question.

1.   When the words, *"This is My body"* and *"this is My blood"* are used, the Lord Jesus Christ was using a metaphor, meaning, *"This represents My body,"* *"This is a picture of My body"* *"This illustrates My body."* The words, *"This is My body"* in the King James Bible occur 4 times in the New Testament. In 1 Corinthians 11:24; In Matthew 26:26; In Mark 14:22; and In Luke 22:19. It would have been impossible for the Living Lord Jesus Christ to say the bread and the cup were literally His body and His blood. That would be impossible since He was there in bodily form. He must have used a metaphor there. We should do the same in 1 Corinthians 11:24. It is clearly a metaphor.

One definition of a metaphor is:

> *"a figure of speech containing an implied comparison, in which a word or phrase ordinarily and primarily used of one thing is applied to another (Examples: the curtain of night, all the world is a stage): cf. simile, mixed metaphor.)*

2.   1 Corinthians 11:29 gives a serious warning not to partake of this ordinance *"unworthily."* I believe this warns against unsaved people partaking of the Lord's Table. It also warns against saved people with known unconfessed sin partaking. Because of disorderly behavior during the Lord's Table in the church of Corinth, many were weak, sickly, and some *"sleep,"* that is, died.

8. Questions About The Dean Burgon Society (DBS)
How to Join The DBS
QUESTION #957
How do you join the Dean Burgon Society (DBS)?
ANSWER #957
You don't need a Th.B. or any degree in order to join the DBS, but I'm glad you have this learning. Here's some the things you need to do in order to join the DBS:
1. Read the ARTICLES OF FAITH
   http://www.deanburgonsociety.org/DBS_Society/articles.htm
2. At the last page of these ARTICLES, you'll see the words, *"Click here for our Membership and Subscription Form."* Follow the directions on this form.
3. Mail it into the Dean Burgon Society.

The Dean Burgon Society Purpose
QUESTION #958
What is the purpose of the Dean Burgon Society?
ANSWER #958
The Dean Burgon Society (DBS) is an organization whose motto is "**IN DEFENSE OF TRADITIONAL BIBLE TEXTS.**" It has been in existence since 1978. It defends in a proper manner the King James Bible and the preserved original Hebrew, Aramaic, and Greek Words on which it is based. It differs from and exposes those English translations and other language translations which are not based on the proper Hebrew, Aramaic, and Greek Words and which use improper texts, improper translators, improper techniques of translation, and improper theology. One of the main distinctives of the DBS today is that it rejects the "*inspiration*" in any sense of the term for the King James Bible or any translation. "*Inspiration*" is reserved exclusively for the Hebrew, Aramaic, and Greek Words underlying the King James Bible. For more details on the work and ministry of the DBS, you can go to its website and look at more of its various purposes and goals: DeanBurgonSociety.org.

Textus Receptus the Last Word?

QUESTION #959

Dean Burgon did not think the Textus Receptus is the last word on the Greek Text, whereas you seemingly do believe that. To that extent, the Dean Burgon Society seems to have taken a position that John William Burgon would be unhappy about. Does therefore the Dean Burgon Society misrepresent Burgon, inasmuch as onlookers would naturally infer that you and Burgon have an identical attitude to the Greek Text? Having said that, I am not saying I believe you are wrong on the textual issue, only that it seems unfair to Burgon's memory to have a fundamentally different basis to your Constitution than Burgon himself could accept.

ANSWER #959

You are partially wrong on Dean Burgon's views. He said no major revision of the Textus Receptus or the King James Bible should be made until <u>all</u> the evidence has been brought forth. That evidence could not be brought forth in Dean Burgon's day and much less can it be brought forth in our day. From his book on *The Traditional Text*, it is written:

> *"Our Readers cannot have yet forgotten his virtual admission that, "Beyond all question the __Textus Receptus__ is the dominant Graeco-Syrian Text of A.D. 350 to A.D. 400. Obtained from a variety of sources, this Text proves to be essentially the same in all. That it requires Revision in respect of many of its lesser details, is undeniable: but it is at least as certain that it is an __excellent Text as it stands,__ __and that the use of it will never lead critical students of__ __Scripture seriously astray__,--which is what no one will venture to predicate concerning any single Critical Edition of the N. T. which has been published since the days of Griesbach, by the disciples of Griesbach's school." (p. 269, The Revision Revised, by Dean John William Burgon).*

Since the evidence has not <u>all</u> been adduced (and Burgon said it couldn't all be adduced in his day, much less in our day), the Dean Burgon Society just as Dean Burgon from his quote above, stands for the Textus Receptus that underlies the King James Bible "__as it stands__."

The DBS and the ESV
QUESTION #960

I am wondering if any of the speakers at the upcoming Dean Burgon Society (DBS) meeting will be addressing the problem of the English Standard Version (ESV)?

ANSWER #960

Though the English Standard Version (ESV) has not yet been taken up at our Dean Burgon Society meetings, we recognize it as an important topic and I will urge one of our DBS speakers to speak about it at one of our meetings in these coming years.

Cassidy's Heretical KJB Position
QUESTION #961

Here is my attempt to define the Traditional Text with a few additional paragraphs to help the reader understand translation. Thomas Cassidy's paper *"The Textual Position of Dean John William Burgon* (1998)" was used as a reference and a help to put this together. Is this definition and explanation satisfactory for publication?

ANSWER #961

Though there might be some of his paper that is accurate, I would not trust Thomas Cassidy's work on this subject. He dropped out of our Dean Burgon Society and has been very critical of it in his various blogs. The most serious error that he holds is his heretical position that the King James Bible was *"inspired of God"* rather than merely being a true, reliable, and accurate English translation.

9. Questions About Catholicism

Catholics Remaining in Church
QUESTION #962

I have a question on Roman Catholics. Can a Roman Catholic be saved and born-again and still remain in the church for a while until they see it is wrong to stay in it? Or is it impossible to be saved and remain in the Church.

ANSWER #962

It is possible to be genuinely saved and born-again and remain in the Roman Catholic Church, but a saved person who is obedient to the Bible, will come out of the Roman Catholic Church as soon as he or she understands Biblical Separation from false doctrines.

No Purgatory at Death
QUESTION #963

I am continually going back and forth regarding my beliefs with a very committed Roman Catholic. I try to gently correct him and show him what the Bible clearly teaches. I was hoping you could give me some verses to show Jim that once a person dies, his soul immediately goes to either Heaven to be with Christ if he is genuinely saved, or to Hell if he has not genuinely received the Lord Jesus Christ as Saviour. Also, can you show how it is too late to pray for people after their death if they are unsaved?

ANSWER #963

Here are a few verses showing saved people go immediately to Heaven without purgatory or anything else:

Philippians 1:23 "*For I am in a strait betwixt two, having a desire **to depart, and to be with Christ**; which is far better:*"

2 Corinthians 5:8 "*We are confident, I say, and willing rather to be **absent from the body, and to be present with the Lord**.*"

Luke 16:19-31 shows what happens to those who die without being saved through genuine faith in the Lord Jesus Christ. Once death comes, there is no turning back, nor is it possible to warn others not to come to the Lake of fire.

19 There was a certain rich man, which was clothed in purple and fine linen, and fared sumptuously every day:
20 And there was a certain beggar named Lazarus, which was laid at his gate, full of sores,
21 And desiring to be fed with the crumbs which fell from the rich man's table: moreover the dogs came and licked his sores.
22 And it came to pass, that the beggar died, and was carried by the angels into Abraham's bosom: the rich man also died, and was buried;
*23 **And in hell he lift up his eyes, being in torments**, and seeth Abraham afar off, and Lazarus in his bosom.*
24 And he cried and said, Father Abraham, have mercy on me, and send Lazarus, that he may dip the tip of his finger in water, and cool my tongue; for I am tormented in this

flame.

25 But Abraham said, Son, remember that thou in thy lifetime receivedst thy good things, and likewise Lazarus evil things: but now he is comforted, and thou art tormented.

26 And beside all this, between us and you there is a great gulf fixed: so that they which would pass from hence to you cannot; neither can they pass to us, that would come from thence.

27 Then he said, I pray thee therefore, father, that thou wouldest send him to my father's house:

28 For I have five brethren; that he may testify unto them, lest they also come into this place of torment.

29 Abraham saith unto him, They have Moses and the prophets; let them hear them.

30 And he said, Nay, father Abraham: but if one went unto them from the dead, they will repent.

31 And he said unto him, If they hear not Moses and the prophets, neither will they be persuaded, though one rose from the dead.

10. Questions About The Textus Receptus

The Date of NT Greek Words

QUESTION #964

I have been told that the Alexandrian texts are the oldest, from the 2nd century, while the majority texts are from the 12th century. Did the person telling me this mislead me in any degree? Can you folks help me chase the truth on this down please?

ANSWER #964

You have been mislead in various ways as to the date of our New Testament Greek Words. First, the so-called Gnostic Critical Alexandrian texts of Vatican and Sinai were not *"from the 2nd century,"* but 200 years later, from the 4th century. Second, it is a false implication to state that *"the majority texts* [including the Textus Receptus Words underlying our KJB] *are from the 12th century."* It is true that the **material** on which the Greek Words of the New Testament books were written down (whether leather, parchment, or some other material) is older in the Gnostic Critical texts found in the Vatican and Sinai manuscripts. However, though the **material** on which the Greek

Words of the New Testament books were written down is not as old and is more recent, the Words found in the Traditional Received text underlying our King James Bible are older than the words found in the Gnostic Critical Greek texts of the Vatican and Sinai manuscripts. As can be shown by various means, the Traditional Received Greek New Testament Words underlying our King James Bible go all the way back to the Apostolic writings themselves. This issue revolves around the **material** the Words were written on versus the Words themselves.

> The Gnostic Critical Greek Vatican and Sinai manuscripts were never circulated or used by the Christians, but were kept in libraries in Egypt where the climate was favorable for their preservation. Both disuse and the climate preserved the **material** on which those words were written. Because Christians used the manuscripts on which the Traditional Words underlying the King James Bible were used daily, they had to be re-copied frequently. These manuscripts were also destroyed when Roman persecutions killed these Christians. This explains the relative ages of the **material**, but not the ages of the Words that were written on that **material**.

Greek Versus Latin In the N.T.
QUESTION #965
Also, when the Textus Receptus was produced, did any of the men such as Erasmus, Stephens, etc. include certain Latin manuscripts in their collations? If so, could we not say that Latin played a major role in the formation of the Traditional Text, not just Hebrew and Greek? Granted, only the Hebrew and Greek were Originals, and the Latin manuscripts were simply copies, as I think everyone agrees, but the point is that we ought not forget to mention the Latin, whatever part it had in the formation of the traditional Text.

ANSWER #965
Where are you getting this Latin emphasis for the N.T.? Is it from Roman Catholic sources? Is it from the Critical Text men? Is it from friends in your country there? Why must we make any mention at all of Latin sources for the development of the New Testament? Why are you defending this so strongly? Are you quoting from someone's books, articles, recordings, or such?

http://en.wikipedia.org/wiki/List_of_New_Testament_Latin_manuscripts
This LINK lists about 96 Old Latin manuscripts. That is a small number compared to the more than 5,500 Greek manuscripts. Certainly these translations in Latin can bear witness to the Greek text from which they were translated, but only as witnesses, not as sources. We must keep these things

distinct and separated. Some today are wrongly saying that our New Testament had its source in Latin or Aramaic rather than in Greek. This error must be opposed and exposed. Thank you for asking this question.

Which Received Text Is Best?

QUESTION #966

What is the essential difference between the Scrivener Greek New Testament edition you have put out, the Novum Testamentum by Jimenez, and the Stephanus A.D. 1550? Which would you recommend?

ANSWER #966

I recommend Scrivener's Greek New Testament edition. I believe the edition of Scrivener's Greek Words are the very Words of the original Greek New Testament. It is based primarily on Beza's 5th Greek New Testament edition of 1598. After studying this question from 1972 to the present, this is my position both on the basis of the **facts** that I have studied from many sources, and also on the basis of my personal **faith**. That edition represents the Greek Traditional Text editions from Erasmus in 1516 for the next 82 years until 1598, when Beza compiled his 5th edition. During this span of time, the Greek text of the Complutensian Polyglot edition and the Greek edition of Stephens were improved in spelling and documentation. It gives the evidence of the over Complutensian Polyglot preserved up to 1967 which is over 99% of the 5,255 MSS. As of now, the number of preserved Greek manuscripts has risen to 5,500 or more. Dean Burgon and other writers have brought me to this trust in the so-called "Traditional Text" which has had a continuity from the Apostolic times to the present. This cannot be said of the Gnostic Critical Greek Text of the Vatican and Sinai family of manuscripts which stopped being copied after around 500 or 600 A.D. They were not copied because the churches knew them to be false witnesses to the New Testament Greek text. Because of the changes made by the Gnostics in Alexandria, Egypt, where they arose, they contain at least 356 false doctrinal passages. I believe that Scrivener's edition differs from the Stephens 1550 edition in approximately 150 small ways.

11. Questions About Billy Graham
Is He A 33rd Degree Mason?

QUESTION #967

Do you still have up-to-date information about the Rev. Billy Graham being a 33rd degree Mason? If this is true and more information seems to be leaking out, I find this to be very sad indeed. A verse of Scripture reads as follows. "*Let God be true and every man a liar.*"

ANSWER #967

We still have the two items on Billy Graham's 33rd degree mason connection as in the catalog: (1) **BFT #2241** (4 pp. @ 5/$1.50 + $4.00 S&H) entitled: *Billy Graham--A 33rd Degree Freemason?* It is by F. Springmeier. And (2) **BFT #2307** (14 pp. @ $1.50 + $3.00 S&H) entitled *Billy Graham, A 33rd Degree Freemason?* It is by Dr. S. H. Tow from Singapore. These can be ordered by these numbers from our BFT Webstore by going to our website at http://www.biblefortoday. org/search.asp if you wish them.

Billy Graham and Universalism?

QUESTION #968

2 Peter 2:1 talks about false teachers. One example of a false teacher today is Billy Graham who has indicated on one TV show that he now believes in some kind of universalism. What does this mean about Billy Graham's own salvation? Also someone mentions that Billy Graham is a 33rd Degree Mason. Is this a fact and if it is true then what is the implication?

ANSWER #968

2 Peter 2:1 teaches that Christ died for the sins of even false teachers. It does not mean these false teachers necessarily accept Christ as the payment for their sins. It does not teach universalism, but it teaches Christ's unlimited atonement for the sins of the world, just as in many other verses.

Only the Lord knows the spiritual condition of Billy Graham. On a television program with Robert Schuler, he intimated that all the heathen were saved and didn't need to trust Christ. I heard him say that myself on a TV broadcast that people in foreign lands who never accepted Christ as their Saviour would go to Heaven. That is serious false teaching! In addition to that, he does not teach or believe that saved people should be separate from apostasy such as Roman Catholicism or apostate Protestantism.

According to documentation that I have read, it is true that Billy Graham is a 33rd degree mason. I read many years ago that he was a 33rd degree mason, but they have probably taken this off the Internet by now.

12. Other Miscellaneous Topics
(1) Questions About Some Tools That Christians Use

Bible Dictionaries

QUESTION #969

What Bible dictionary would you recommend as a companion to the King James Bible?

ANSWER #969

Though there are some things within it that I differ with, I think that *Unger's Bible Dictionary* is the best to date. It was originally written by my Hebrew professor at Dallas Theological Seminary (1948-1953), Dr. Merrill F. Unger. It has been revised since Dr. Unger's death and has kept up with current developments in the area of the Bible and related subjects. Just use it with discernment. For example, he did not stand for the Textus Receptus and the King James Bible, following the false position of Dallas Theological Seminary in these areas.

Lexicons and Concordances

QUESTION #970

What do you think is a good lexicon and a concordance that has Greek and Hebrew information? What do you think about the interlinear Greek and Hebrew ones?

ANSWER #970

I prefer Strong's Concordance to Vine's since it is more complete and has all the Hebrew and Greek words in it. I recommend for lexicons: (1) *The Analytical Hebrew Lexicon* and (2) *The New Analytical Greek Lexicon*. I recommend for concordances with Hebrew and Greek in them: (1) *Englishman's Hebrew Concordance* and (2) *Englishman's Greek Concordance*. For interlinear Hebrew and Greek Bibles, there is one published by Jay Green which combines both the Old Testament and the New Testament. Though it might not be accurate in all its translations of the Hebrew and Greek Words, at least you can see which Hebrew or Greek Word is behind the English words and you can look them up independently in sound lexicons.

Vine's Word Studies

QUESTION #971

In examining *Vine's Word Studies* some years ago, I found that it had words based on the RSV and NIV, in other words, Westcott and Hort. Do you have any articles on Vine's book? My Sunday School teacher said all the fundamentalist churches use Vine's, not Strong's. Can you please help me?

ANSWER #971

I don't have any articles on *Vine's Word Studies*, but I know he was a follower of the Gnostic Critical Greek Text. That false text differs from our Received Greek New Testament Text in over 8,000 places. This includes 356 doctrinal passages that are in error. If you look at the introductory pages of Vine's book, I believe his textual base is given. The original *Strong's Concordance* was based on the Received Text underlying the King James Bible. Later editions of Strong's have changed many things, but I believe it is still based on the Received Text. I would strongly recommend Strong's over Vine's.

The Works of Kenneth Wuest

QUESTION #972

What information do you have on the background of Kenneth Wuest and his work? I'd greatly appreciate any & all guidance you provide.

ANSWER #972

Dr. Kenneth Wuest was a nice gentleman. I visited his Greek class when visiting my wife who attended Moody Bible Institute before we were married. At the time, I didn't know anything about the two Greek texts. I took Wuest's word about the various books he had recommended and bought them all. When I knew the truth about the two Greek texts, I discovered all of his recommended books were based on the Gnostic Critical Greek New Testament text, so I have ceased using them. Wuest has a number of good word pictures in his word-picture book, but beware of his erroneous Gnostic Critical Greek Text that he loved.

(2) Questions About Pastor John MacArthur

MacArthur's Heresy the Blood

QUESTION #973

Also, right now I am listening to your message about Peter and defense of the Word. During it you again mentioned MacArthur's heresy. Last Sunday, during our adult Bible class, and during the discussion of the Old Testament blood sacrifices, someone mentioned that it was not the literal blood shed on the cross. I spoke up and said that was heresy and mentioned the fact that this sounds like John MacArthur's heresy. The leader then stepped in and said, "let's not discuss that right now." So I said nothing further.

But after our Wednesday night prayer meeting, the pastor told me that I should not have raised the subject of MacArthur's heresy because he believes that the King James Bible Fundamentalists are interpreting Christ's blood "too literal." I asked him how he knew what I said in that class when he was not even present. He told me that one of the women in the class had expressed concern about what I had said. It was just another example of my being divisive and speaking things that were untrue. I asked the pastor, who is a graduate of Bob Jones University and Calvary Baptist Seminary, why she did not come to me after the class if she was concerned? He had no response.

Please pray for me because, after 16 years of faithful attendance and financial support of this Baptist Church, I believe I must seek a King James Bible-believing church to attend and support for the rest of my life on this earth.

ANSWER #973

I'm sorry to hear of your problem with telling the TRUTH about John MacArthur's heresy on the blood of Christ. I used to go to that Baptist church when I was a Navy Chaplain on active duty. The pastor's being a graduate both from Bob Jones University and Calvary Baptist Seminary explains how he is loyal to the Gnostic Critical Greek text just as MacArthur is.

May the Lord lead you in finding a good King James Bible church. You can listen to our church if you have an Internet at BibleForToday.org LIVE Sundays at 10 a.m. and 1:30 p.m. (Eastern Time) on the BROWN BOX, and by recording the rest if the week on the YELLOW BOX. All our services and messages are given on that site 24 hours a day, 7 days a week as I present verse by verse messages from Romans through Revelation on a 16-week circuit.

"I Must Work" or "He Must Work"
QUESTION #974

I just heard a sermon from John MacArthur on John 9:4. He said that, the Textus Receptus has "*I must work . . .* " He said that in the other texts, the "*I*" has been replaced with "*we*." MacArthur says that he likes "*we*" instead of "*I*." What do you think of this? What problems are there if it reads "*we*" instead of "*I*" ?

ANSWER #974

John 9:4 "*I must work the works of him that sent me, while it is day: the night cometh, when no man can work.*"

You are correct. The Textus Receptus Greek text has "*I*," and the Gnostic Critical Text has "*we*." John MacArthur is a strong believer in this perverted Gnostic Critical Text, so it is understandable that he follows it in this verse, and thus makes it "*we*." MacArthur is in error in this matter, and in many, many others as well. He has a mixture of truth and error. I would caution you, either not to listen to him or read after him at all, or, if you do, use extreme caution as you seek to sift carefully between his truths and his errors.

For the strong evidence in favor of "*I*" (EGO) as opposed to "*we*," (HEMEIS), I recommend that you consult page 215 of Dr. Jack Moorman's excellent book, *Early Manuscripts, Church Fathers, and the Authorized Version.* It is **BFT #3230** @ $20.00 + $8.00 S&H. He gives the documented authorities on both sides of this issue with the stronger side for "*I.*"

(3) Questions About Bob Jones University

BJU Graduates and the LXX
QUESTION #975

Hello, I was talking to a Bob Jones University graduate regarding the Bible versions. He touched on a question that I wasn't completely sure on my answer. Here are two New Testament passages that he gave me with their corresponding Old Testament passage: Acts 15:16-17 with Amos 9:11-12. And Romans 3:10-18 with Psalm 14:1-7.

In his argument he said that the Old Testament passage referred to in the New Testament reads the same as the Septuagint. He claimed that the Hebrew Masoretic text was not used by the King James translators. He also said that

maybe the original writers of Scripture were using the Septuagint. He seemed to think that this validated the modern versions.

ANSWER #975

I don't think you're going to make much headway with this Bob Jones University graduate Ph.D. The first question is I would have for him is, does he really want to search out the truth and know it, or does he just want to convince you that what he was taught at Bob Jones University is correct? If the latter, I wouldn't waste any of your time on him on this issue.

1. The Septuagint (LXX) was not even in existence from Genesis through Malachi B.C. No one has produced the entire Old Testament in Greek that existed B.C. Until this has been done, I will not believe the LXX existed B.C. There might be a few Old Testament books in Greek B.C., but not the entire Old Testament. The LXX, as such, was not in existence until Origen put it in his six-column *Hexapla* in the A.D. 200's. If the words are similar or the same, it is quite possible that the LXX quoted from the New Testament rather than the reverse.

---

2. God the Holy Spirit Who gave the Words of the Old Testament and Words of the New Testament is sovereign, and He is able to change any of the Words He wishes to for His own purposes.

3. The literal and exact precise Words he assumes came from the LXX are not the exact, precise words, but have a variant or two in each quote. If it's not an exact quotation, it is not a quotation at all, but a only a slight modification of the Hebrew Words.

Dr. Kirk DiVietro has written a book on this called *Did Jesus and the Apostles Quote the Septuagint*? It can be obtained as **BFT #2707, 53 pages, @ $5.50 + $6.00 S&H.**

---

(4) Questions About Angels
Michael the Archangel
QUESTION #976

Was Michael the Archangel a created being? I have a dispute from a Seventh Day Adventist. He believes that. But the Seventh Day Adventists teach that Michael was not a created being. They teach that he was Jesus Christ. What is your opinion?

ANSWER #976

Jude 9: *"Yet **Michael the archangel**, when contending with the devil he disputed about the body of Moses, durst not*

bring against him a railing accusation, but said, The Lord rebuke thee."

Revelation 12:7: *"And there was war in heaven: **Michael and his angels** fought against the dragon; and the dragon fought and his angels,"*

From these two Bible verses where Michael is mentioned, it is clear that Michael was an angel. He is not the Lord Jesus Christ. As such, Michael was a created being. He was created when all the other angels were created in Genesis 1:1: *"In the beginning God created the heaven and the earth."* It is assumed that the *"angels"* were part of what God created in *"the heaven."*

"When the morning stars sang together, And all the sons of God shouted for joy?" (Job 38:7) This is speaking of God's creation of the world. The *"sons of God"* in Job refers to the angels. Evidently they had been created prior to God's creation of the world and were witnesses of that creation.

The Angel at Christ's Birth
QUESTION #977
In Luke 2:9-10, the angel that announced the birth of the Lord Jesus Christ was not named. Wasn't Michael the angel of Israel? Wouldn't he be the logical one to make this announcement?
ANSWER #977
Yes, it could have been Michael. But since it is not named, we should be cautious in our speculations about this.

Were Angels in Genesis 6?
QUESTION #978
My last pastor and the one before him taught that fallen angels were having sex with women in Genesis 6. I believe, as long as I can remember I never took this to being truth from what I read in the Bible. I did a study and I believe differently. These women had sex with men of renown who were earthly sinners. I always believed, from the New Testament that angels don't have sex.
ANSWER #978
Jude 1:6 "*And the **angels which kept not their first estate, but left their own habitation**, he hath reserved in everlasting chains under darkness unto the judgment of the great day.*"

I believe this verse is a reference to what took place in Genesis 6. These creatures are called the "*sons of God.*" If you check all the other references to the "*sons of God,*" you will find that they refer to angels. I believe all 5 occurrences of "*sons of God*" in the books of Genesis and Job refer to angels, either fallen or holy. God had to bring on the flood to prevent these giants (NEPHALIM) or "*fallen ones*" to pollute the human race and prevent the line a pure human race to eventually bring on the Messiah, the Lord Jesus Christ, to redeem the ones who genuinely trust Him.

(5) Questions About Dean John William Burgon
Burgon's Early Church Fathers
QUESTION #979
I have heard it said that Burgon made a list of thousands of quotations from the Early Church Fathers that would enable nearly all of the New

Testament to be reconstructed. Do you know where I can find a list of these? I am particularly interested in references to the Gospels in the Early Church Fathers.

ANSWER #979

Dean John W. Burgon compiled an index of over 186,000 quotations from the Early Church Fathers. They are in the British museum and have never been published. Dr. Jack Moorman has examined these quotations and determined that they are not able to be published since they are color-coded. To publish in color would be very expensive. Also, the British Museum is now charging a high amount per page to copy them. In addition to this, you would have to have the same edition of the church fathers that Burgon had in order for you to find the quotation. These editions are no longer available. However, Dr. Moorman has reconstructed some of the same quotations. His study is available as **BFT #3230** @ $20.00 + $7.00 S&H. It is called *EARLY MANUSCRIPTS, CHURCH FATHERS, AND THE AUTHORIZED VERSION.*

I do not believe, however, as some have said, that with these quotes from the Church Fathers, the entire Greek New Testament could be reconstructed. I believe that is false and should not be relied upon.

Dean Burgon As an Anglican
QUESTION #980

I've recommended your ministry to someone. They sent me the following link.   http://en.wikipedia.org/wiki/Dean_Burgon.   They are questioning the opening statement in which is says Mr. Burgon was an English Anglican divine. They also sent this link about being an English Anglican Divine.http://en.wikipedia.org/wiki/AnglicanismAnglican_divines

*"John William Burgon (21 August 1813 – 4 August 1888) was an **English Anglican divine** who become the Dean of Chichester Cathedral in 1876. He is remembered for his passionate defense of the historicity and Mosaic authorship of Genesis and of Biblical inerrancy in general."*

Also, why does this listing state Dean Burgon's name as John William?

ANSWER #980

This is Dean Burgon's full name. Dean John William Burgon was indeed an *"Anglican"* that is, a member of the Church of England. That is correct. We don't necessarily agree with Burgon's Anglicanism (I am a Baptist), but the Dean Burgon Society stands with him in his defense of the Traditional Greek Text of the New Testament, his vigorous exposure of the false Gnostic Critical Greek Text promulgated by his fellow Anglicans, Bishop

Westcott and Professor Hort, and his sound defense of the King James Bible
as over against the false English Revised Version of 1881. We have reprinted
five of his books, all of which are excellent and well documented in these
above areas.

(6) Questions About Music
QUESTION #981

My wife and I have recently been listening to your services and finding
them to be edifying. We live in a small East Texas town and stopped attending
our local church because of the many changes that reflect modernism in
today's church. They don't use the King James Bible nor sing from traditional
hymn books. The church is over a 100 years old, but has continued to evolve
with the culture and clearly has fallen away as they have forgotten their first
love. We have tried to bring this to their attention but it's leaders continue on
a self-serving mission to gain new members and pervert grace.

I'm inquiring on purchasing a hymnal, but do not see it available on your
website. May I purchase one of these? I've also been told that your *Defined
King James Bible* is a must! Would you have this in large print? Praise God
for your church's ministry.

ANSWER #981

I am very pleased that you have been attending our services here at the
Bible for Today Baptist Church in Collingswood, New Jersey and have
found them to be edifying. I understand very well your situation. Many of our
friends have experienced the same thing with their local churches. They have
different Bibles, different music, different standards, and many other different
things. We welcome you to our ministry through the Internet. If you send us
your address, we would be glad to send you a copy of our hymn book so you
can follow along with our hymns during our services.

We take care of sending out our *Defined King James Bible*. We have it
in genuine leather medium print (10-point type) at about 6" x 8" size @ **$35.00**
+$7.00 S&H (hardback is **$15.00 + S&H**). We also have it in genuine leather
large print (12-point type) at about 9" x 11" size @ **$40.00 +$7.00 S&H**.
(hardback is **$20.00 +S&H**). There is a choice of colors of either black or
burgundy.

(7) Questions About The Greek Orthodox Church

QUESTION #982

I was just reading an article of the Greek Orthodox Church. It says that this church does not believe that every word in the Bible was dictated by God. They do not believe the Bible is free from error concerning the facts about science, history, geology, biology, etc. They have 49 books in the Old Testament rather than 39. Is this teaching correct?

ANSWER #982

Every one of these things that are you mentioned in your question are in error. In addition to these, there are many other things taught by the Greek Orthodox Church that are also in error. Some of their doctrinal beliefs can be found at http://orthodoxinfo.com/general/doctrine1.aspx if you wish to look at them.

(8) Questions About The Trinitarian Bible Society

QUESTION #983

I would like your advice and opinion please: in your experience, how does the Trinitarian Bible Society stand? Are they worthy of support, membership, etc.?

ANSWER #983

The Trinitarian Bible Society (TBS) prints the proper Scrivener's Greek Text which underlies the King James Bible and the King James Bible for which we are grateful. Unfortunately, some of the foreign Bible translations they print do not conform close enough to the Hebrew, Aramaic, and Greek Words underlying the King James Bible. At one point in their history, they were almost ready to publish the New King James Version, but I am glad to say that this suggestion was stopped several years ago. To my knowledge, the only English version they publish is the King James Bible. I am grateful for this.

Theologically, as a Baptist, I would differ regarding three areas: (1) they have a strong hyper-Calvinist position; (2) they lack a proper practice of Bible separation from apostasy and compromise; and (3) some of the foreign translations that they print do not always conform accurately to the New Testament Textus Receptus underlying the King James Bible.

Having said all of this, though we differ on some things, we are glad for their good Greek New Testament and various King James Bible publications.

I know their General Secretary and have had fellowship with him. He visited us when he was here several months ago. Mrs. Waite and I also visited him and the Trinitarian Bible Society headquarters when in London several years ago. They are certainly very much better than either the American, the British, or the United Bible Societies that do not stand for the proper Hebrew, Aramaic, or Greek texts or for the King James Bible. As to what you should do in support of the Trinitarian Bible Society, the Lord will have to lead you in your decisions in this area.

(9) Questions About The Meaning of The "Scriptures"

QUESTION #984

I have a question about your statement that *"Scriptures"* usually only refers to the Old Testament. In 2 Peter 3:16 the term, *"other Scriptures,"* referring to Paul's epistles, establishes that they also are *"Scriptures."* Do you agree?

ANSWER #984

I agree that this verse establishes that, since Paul's epistles are GRAPHE (*"scripture"*), all of the New Testament Greek Words are also *"scripture"* (GRAPHE).

Here is a complete list found in the Greek New Testament underlying the King James Bible where the word GRAPHE (*"scripture"*) is used 51 times. In every instance, it refers back either to the original Hebrew Old Testament, or the original Greek New Testament. It never refers, nor should it ever be used to refer to any translation of the Hebrew, Aramaic, or Greek Words, no matter what language is involved.

1. Matthew 21:42 "never read the scriptures"
2. Matthew 22:29 "not knowing the scripture"
3. Matthew 26:54 "the scriptures be fulfilled"
4. Matthew 26:56 "scriptures of the prophets"
5. Mark 12:10 "read this scripture the stone"
6. Mark 12:24 "know not the scriptures"
7. Mark 14:49 "the scriptures must be fulfilled"
8. Mark 15:28 "And the scripture was fulfilled,"
9. Luke 4:21 "this scripture fulfilled in your ears."
10. Luke 24:27 "in all the scriptures the things"
11. Luke 24:32 "He opened to us the scriptures"
12. Luke 24:45 "might understand the scriptures"
13. John 2:22 "they believed the scripture,"

14. John 5:39 "search the scriptures"
15. John 7:38 "as the scripture hath said,"
16. John 7:42 "Hath not the scripture said,"
17. John 10:35 "the scripture cannot be broken;"
18. John 13:18 "the scripture may be fulfilled,"
19. John 17:12 "the scripture might be fulfilled."
20. John 19:24 "the scripture might be fulfilled,"
21. John 19:28 "the scripture might be fulfilled,"
22. John 19:36 "the scripture should be fulfilled,"
23. John 19:37 "another scripture saith,"
24. John 20:9 "knew not the scripture"
25. Acts 1:16 "this scripture must needs be fulfilled"
26. Acts 18:32 "the place of the scripture"
27. Acts 8:35 "began at the same scripture"
28. Acts 17:2 "out of the scriptures"
29. Acts 17:11 "searched the scriptures"
30. Acts 18:24 "mighty in the scriptures"
31. Acts 18:28 "shewing by the scriptures"
32. Romans 1:2 "in the holy scriptures"
33. Romans 4:3 "what saith the scripture?"
34. Romans 9:17 "the scripture saith"
35. Romans 10:11 "the scripture saith,"
36. Romans 11:2 "what the scripture saith"
37. Romans 15:4 "comfort of the scriptures"
38. Romans 16:26 "the scriptures of the prophets."
39. 1 Cor. 15:3 "according to the scriptures"
40. 1 Cor. 15:4 "according to the scriptures"
41. Galatians 3:8 "And the scripture,"
42. Galatians 3:22 "the scripture hath concluded"
43. Galatians 4:30 "what saith the scripture?"
44. 1 Timothy 5:18 "the scripture saith,"
45. 2 Timothy 3:16 "All scripture is given by inspiration"
46. James 2:8 "according to the scripture"
47. James 2:23 "the scripture was fulfilled"
48. James 4:5 "the scripture saith in vain"
49. 1 Peter 2:6 "contained in the scripture,"
50. 2 Peter 1:20 "prophecy of the scripture"
51. <u>2 Peter 3:16</u> "do also the other scriptures"

2 Peter 3:15–16

15 "*And account that the longsuffering of our Lord is salvation; <u>even as our beloved brother PAUL</u> also*

according to the wisdom given unto him hath written unto you;"

16 *"As also <u>in ALL HIS EPISTLES</u>, speaking in them of these things; in which are some things hard to be understood, which they that are unlearned and unstable wrest, as they do also <u>the OTHER SCRIPTURES</u>, unto their own destruction."*

As I said before, all 51 of these uses of the Greek word, GRAPHE, refer to God's own Words from the Old Testament Hebrew or New Testament Greek Bibles. *"Other scriptures"* in 2 Peter 3:16 identifies Paul's writings (GRAPHE) as also being God's very Words. The point is that *"scripture"* and *"scriptures"* in the New Testament use GRAPHE for the very Words that God Himself gave. **GRAPHE (*"scripture"* or *"scriptures"*) is never used for any translation of those Words in any language of the world, including the King James Bible's English.** Therefore, 2 Timothy 3:16's words, *"All scripture"* (PASA GRAPHE) refer to God's own Words--whether to Old Testament Hebrew or Aramaic Words, or to New Testament Greek Words.

In view of this evidence, the Greek word, GRAPHE, (*"Scripture"*), does not, should not, nor can it ever refer to the King James Bible or any other translation as the Ruckmanites and Riplingerites use it to prove the *"inspiration"* of the King James Bible. They, and others who do the same thing, are totally in error in this.

(10) Questions About Fasting
QUESTION #985

How about fasting for Christians today? Do the following verses teach it for Christians? (1) Acts 14:23; (2) 1 Corinthians7:5; and Mark 2:20?
ANSWER #985

(1)   **Acts 14:23** Fasting was **practiced** by the Apostles, but this is **not a command** to fast in this age of grace for present-day Christians.

Acts 14:23 *"And when they had ordained them elders in every church, and had **prayed with fasting**, they commended them to the Lord, on whom they believed."*

(2)   **1 Corinthians 7:5** .This teaches that Christian couples could fast voluntarily, if they wish, but there is **no New Testament command** for those who are saved in this age of grace that they are obligated to fast.

1 Corinthians 7:5 *"Defraud ye not one the other, except it be with consent for a time, **that ye may give yourselves to fasting and prayer**; and come together again, that Satan* *tempt you not for your incontinency."*

(3)   **Mark 2:20** is talking about the Jewish bridegroom. Yes, fasting was a <u>Jewish custom</u>, but there is **no New Testament command for Christians**.

> **Mark 2:20** *"But the days will come, when the bridegroom shall be taken away from them, and **then shall they fast** in those days."*

Some Bible-believing Christians practice fasting, believing this to be something they should do. They are free to do this from time to time if they wish, but there is **no command in the age of grace** that all saved people should do this as a requirement or even as an ordinance such as baptism and the Lord's supper.

(11) Questions About Easter

QUESTION #986

Is it all right for Christians to celebrate Easter such as the one in April?

ANSWER #986

Christians are at liberty to do as they please about this. But I urge them to search out the roots and background of Easter. It originated from the goddess Ishtar and Astarte with all of its paganism, fornication, and other evil things that were involved in its celebration. I have given a LINK to an article by Dr. Scott Johnson which gives the pagan background of Easter. You can find more information there.   http://www.contendingfortruth.com/?p=1184 There is nothing pagan "Easter" celebrations about the bodily resurrection of the Lord Jesus Christ.

(12) Questions About Drinking

QUESTION #987

I have read and appreciated the course on alcohol from Liberty Baptist Church. It has been very helpful. I recently heard say that the word for "wine" in John 2 is the same word used in Ephesians 5:18 in the context of being *"not drunk."* I also see in Strong's dictionary the words in John 2:10 *"have well drunk"* are shown to be from a Greek word, METHUSKO. That word was defined as *"from another form of G3178; to drink to intoxication, that is, get drunk."* I don't know how to answer this. It seems to support the carnal Christian interpretation that the wine that the Lord made was alcoholic. What can I say to this?

ANSWER #987

John 2:10 reads as follows:

> "*And saith unto him, Every man at the beginning doth set forth good wine; and when men have **well drunk**, then that which is worse: but thou hast kept the good wine until now.*"
> (John 2:10)

Here, the "*governor*" is speaking to the "*bridegroom*" as this feast. He is merely saying what usually happens at such weddings. The men get drunk on good wine that is fermented. When they're all drunk, the host usually serves them bad wine. Being "*well drunk*," they don't know whether it is good or bad. This water which the Lord turned into wine was called "*good wine*." There is nothing here that necessitates that this "*good wine*" that the Lord made was intoxicating. The Lord Jesus Christ created excellent non-fermented grape juice from water by a miracle. This grape juice or non-fermented "*wine*" was given to these "*well drunk*" men. If they were "*drunk*," it was not from drinking the "*good wine*." The "*good wine*" did not make them "*drunk*" nor should it be concluded that it was fermented wine. OINOS is the Greek word used here for "*wine*." It depends on the context whether it is fermented or just grape juice. In this case, it was grape juice.

(13) Questions About Israel

QUESTION #988

I know that there's a Palestinian state today. Has the Palestinian state existed since the Old Testament, or was it invented later?

ANSWER #988

After Israel drove out the Canaanite nations, there was no Palestinian state. That state came in recently. http://en.wikipedia.org/wiki/Palestine gives a historical background of the country of Palestine.

(13) Questions About Our BFT Videos

QUESTION #989

How often is the Bible For Today webpage updated with the most recent videos? I am a Christian hospital chaplain and I can't always experience the services "live." I am very thankful for these videos!

ANSWER #989

I am glad you appreciate the videos of our services. They are updated every Sunday and every Thursday to keep current with our two Sunday services (10 a.m. Eastern and 1:30 p.m. Eastern) and our Thursday service (8 p.m. Eastern). They can be seen LIVE at BibleForToday.org on the **BROWN BOX** at those times. They can be seen RECORDED at the same webpage on the **YELLOW BOX** for the current messages during all of the following week.

(14) Questions About Westcott And Hort

QUESTION #990

I wondered if you could give me some examples of false and heretical teachings from Westcott's *Commentary on the Gospel of John.*

ANSWER #990

That is a task too detailed to answer here. Here's what I suggest you do if you really want to find the specific answers to your question about Westcott's errors in his *Commentary on the Gospel of John* that I referred to in my book, *HERESIES OF WESTCOTT AND HORT* (**BFT #595** @ **$8.00** + **$4.00 S&H**).

1. Go to my book, *HERESIES OF WESTCOTT AND HORT,* on page 4 and see the books where I took these quotes, including *Westcott's Gospel of John.*

2. Then go through the entire book and look for WESTCOTT--JOHN. Circle the quotes that refer to that source and pick the ones you want to use.

3. Under A-2, p. 7 there is a quote.

4. Under A-5, p. 9 there is a quote.

5. Under C-1, p. 9 there is a quote.

6. Under D-1, p. 10, there is a quote, and so on through the book. In this way, you can find the many heretical statements that Westcott mentioned from his *Commentary on the Gospel of John* as well as from his *Commentaries on Hebrews* and *The Epistles of John.*

(15) Questions About Dr. Lewis Sperry Chafer

QUESTION #991

I hear sayings that the late Dr. Chafer had complained about the translation of Hebrews 1:2: "*by whom also he made the **worlds**.*" He believed that it should have been translated "*ages.*" He believed "*ages*" supports better the dispensational doctrine and is one of the meanings of the Greek Word, AION, here. Did the translators of the King James Bible 1611 made a mistake translating AION as "*worlds*" instead of "*ages*"? What's your explanation about this?

ANSWER #991

Though I respect Dr. Lewis Sperry Chafer (one of my teachers for four years at the Dallas Theological Seminary), I would disagree with him somewhat, at least, in this place. Sometimes AION can mean "*world*" in and sometimes it can mean "*ages.*" I don't think it is a major problem.

(16) Questions About James White

QUESTION #992

I thank you for all the research you've done on Bible translation. I'm a young man and have been born-again for about 6 years. I believe that God's living words in English are to be found in the Authorized Version of the Scriptures. I was wondering about a man named Dr. James White. Have you ever debated this man in regards to the Bible translation issue? Is there any good youtube videos or anything that you know of where Dr. James White is challenged by a person such as yourself?

ANSWER #992

We have the following materials on James White. I debated him on the radio for around three hours some years ago.

- BFT #2989 135pp. $11.00 Examining The King James Only Controversy' in Answer to James White by David Cloud

- BFT #3001 Cassette $4.00 Radio Answer to James White's Book on SW Radio, Dr. D. A. Waite and Dr. Larry Spargamino

- BFT #2494/1-2 Cassettes $7.00 Radio Debate on the King James Bible with James White, by Dr. D. A. Waite and James White

- BFT/104-109 Cassettes $18.00 Refuting James White's "KJVO Controversy" (#1-6) by Dr. D. A. Waite

- BFT #2874 56 pp. $5.50 Refuting James White's Lies in his King James Only Book, by David Cloud

BFT #2562 86 pp. $9.00 Why Not the King James Bible!--Answer to KJVO Book, by Dr. Kirk DiVietro

(17) Questions About Witches

QUESTION #993

Someone recently brought to my attention that they read that King James had witches put to death. Is there any validity to this? Is there a resource I can go to?

ANSWER #993

http://scottishhistory.suite101.com/article.cfm/the_berwick_witches The LINK above shows that 200 witches planned to kill King James I. Perhaps he killed them first. You can read the article and find out perhaps. That's all I know about it. The Old Testament law of Moses(which we are not under today) demanded death for witches.

Exodus 22:18 "Thou shalt **not suffer a witch to live.**"

*"**There shall not be found among you** any one that maketh his son or his daughter to pass through the fire, or that useth divination, or an observer of times, or an enchanter, or **a witch**,"*

Perhaps this is why these witches were killed by misapplying this verse to the New Testament teaching. [*"Thou shalt **not suffer a witch to live**." (Exodus 22:18)]

It is wrong to assume that King James I was a good king. He did much evil to many people during his reign. The LINK below shows some of these evils. http://one-evil.org/content/people_17c_james_i.html

King James I also persecuted the Puritans and the Pilgrims who didn't go along with the established Church of England as detailed in the LINK below.

http://www.mainlesson.com/display.php?author=evans&book=america&story=pilgrims

(18) Questions About Schools

QUESTION #994

I would like your opinion on Andersonville Theological Seminary. Do you believe they are a reputable school?

ANSWER #994

I looked up the school on the Internet. Though I found a caption called *"philosophy,"* I saw no doctrinal statement as to what beliefs this school holds to. This makes me wonder what they believe. Are they ashamed of what they believe? I could not recommend this school unless and until I was able to see what doctrines they believe.

(19) Questions About Salvation

QUESTION #995

I have been saved for about 25 years and have just recently began to devote myself fully to Christ and started attending meetings. I became very confused as to whether I am really saved or if I am only saved in my head and not in my heart. I wonder if I am really saved. I believe 100% in God's Words, the King James Bible, and I stand firm to everything that was taught to me and everything I've learned in the Bible.

I have been a smoker for about 26 years. I think that this sin is so great that it is stopping me from having the salvation I need. I've tried to quit many, many times. I have prayed about it many times. Can this be the whole cause of my conscience and can it be so that I was never saved in the first place? Does that mean that I have no other chance to be saved?

ANSWER #995

I am sorry you are not sure of your salvation. This is very important to be assured of. Though smoking is bad for you, it can't make you lose your salvation if you once have it.

Because your problem is so complicated, I believe the best way for me to help you is for us to talk on the phone about some of these things, and look at the Bible for its simple, but sure, way of salvation for us sinners. You can call me at **856-854-4747** and we can talk about all of these things. If you do not have an unlimited line, I can call you back. It won't cost you anything that way. In the meantime, I urge you (if you have an internet with fast speed) to tune into our church services at BibleForToday.org. Click the BROWN BOX and you can hear preaching verse by verse from Romans through Revelation on a 16-week basis. This might help you in this matter.

(20) Questions About Prayer

QUESTION #996

I, my wife, and her son have just listened to a sermon by you on Romans. Her son has a question for you. I can't answer for you, so I suggested he ask you about it. I will let him ask you in his own words. I was just wondering why when you pray why do you speak in old English saying thee, thy, and thou? I was wondering if there is any particular reason for it or if it was just your preference?

ANSWER #996

I pray to the Lord using THEE, THY, and THOU, because it is a very personal use of the singular pronoun, "YOU." It shows respect and close relationship. I use these terms only for the Lord, never for human beings. I make a distinction between God and man in this way. These are terms of respect and of differentiation between God and man. I believe this is why the King James Bible translators used these terms for the Lord. It Is like the Spanish used of TU rather than USTED when speaking of the Lord or close friends in second person singular. USTED is formal and distant. It is used of those the person does not know well. TU is personal and indicates a close and intimate relationship between two people. This is why it is used when praying to the Lord.

(21) Questions About Baptism

QUESTION #997

I recently heard someone say that all the translators of the King James Bible believed in infant baptism. It wasn't mentioned as though that disqualified them from being faithful translators, but do you know whether or not that's an accurate statement?

ANSWER #997

Without knowing details, since every one of the King James Bible translators was a member of the Church of England, I would assume that 100% of them believed in infant baptism by sprinkling since that is the usual method of baptism in the Anglican church. We, as Baptists, disagree with that method of baptism, believing in baptism by immersion of only genuinely saved and born-again people. However, the translators' method of baptism had nothing whatsoever with their skills and abilities that they possessed in doing their excellent King James Bible translation.

(22) Questions About the Apocrypha

Resources About the Apocrypha

QUESTION #998

Thank you for your tireless defense of the Word of God. I know at times this is not easy yet the Lord will bless you for all that you do for Him. I have some questions that I would like to ask. If you could point me to resources, I would appreciate this.

(1) What are your thoughts on the Book of Enoch?

(2) What resources do you have on the Apocrypha?

ANSWER #998

(1)   The book of Enoch.

http://en.wikipedia.org/wiki/Book_of_Enoch is a link that gives the background on the book of Enoch. Though a small portion of it is quoted in Jude 1:1-14, the book is not a part of the canonical Scriptures.

(2) The Apocrypha.

http://en.wikipedia.org/wiki/Apocrypha is a link that gives the background of the Apocrypha. Though it was included in the King James Bible in 1611, it is not a part of canonical Scriptures. In my opinion, the 1611 King James Bible should not have included the Apocrypha. It was placed between Malachi and Matthew by them in 1611. Fortunately, it has been removed from the King James Bible, though it is retained in the Roman Catholic versions. I have a cassette tape on *"Why the Apocrypha Should Be Rejected From Our Bibles."* It can be ordered as **BFT #1110 @ $4.00 + $2.00 S&H**.

Apocrypha in the KJB vs. Rome

QUESTION #999

Was there any difference in the way the King James Bible used the Apocrypha and the way the Roman Catholic Bibles use it?

ANSWER #999

The King James Bible separated the Apocrypha from the rest of the Bible books of the Old Testament by placing it after Malachi and before Matthew. The Roman Catholic Bibles intersperse the Apocryphal books in between the regular Bible books, therefore, making no distinction, and considering them all the canonical and of equal value one with another.

Apocrypha & the KJB Translators

QUESTION #1000

What did the King James Bible translators and the Church of England think about the Apocrypha?

ANSWER #1000

In this LINK (http://temple-of-faith.org/lessons/39art.htm) there is a listing of the "*Thirty-Nine Articles of Faith*" of the Church of England. In these Articles, there is an enumeration of the "*canonical*" books of the Old Testament. The 14 books of the Apocrypha are not on that list, but are listed separately. They were not considered "*canonical*" by the Church of England or by the King James Bible translators. The Roman Catholic Church, however, believes that the Apocryphal books are just as "*canonical*" as all the other books of the Bible. I am glad that the King James Bible we use does not have the Apocrypha in it, but I am sorry that the 1611 edition contained it. I believe it was pressure from the king that caused it to be included.

Index of Words And Phrases

About the Author

The author of this book, Dr. D. A. Waite, received a B.A. (Bachelor of Arts) in classical Greek and Latin from the University of Michigan in 1948, a Th.M. (Master of Theology), with high honors, in New Testament Greek Literature and Exegesis from Dallas Theological Seminary in 1952, an M.A. (Master of Arts) in Speech from Southern Methodist University in 1953, a Th.D. (Doctor of Theology), with honors, in Bible Exposition from Dallas Theological Seminary in 1955, and a Ph.D. in Speech from Purdue University in 1961. He holds both New Jersey and Pennsylvania teacher certificates in Greek and Language Arts.

He has been a teacher in the areas of Greek, Hebrew, Bible, Speech, and English for over thirty-five years in ten schools, including one junior high, one senior high, four Bible institutes, two colleges, two universities, and one seminary. He served his country as a Navy Chaplain for five years on active duty; pastored three churches; was Chairman and Director of the Radio and Audio-Film Commission of the American Council of Christian Churches; since 1969, has been Founder, President, and Director of THE BIBLE FOR TODAY; since 1978, has been President of the DEAN BURGON SOCIETY; has produced over 800 other studies, books, audio cassettes, CD's, VCR's, or DVD's on various topics; and is heard on a thirty-minute weekly program, IN DEFENSE OF TRADITIONAL BIBLE TEXTS, on radio, and streaming on the Internet at BibleForToday.org, 24/7/365. •

Dr. and Mrs. Waite have been married since 1948; they have four sons, one daughter, and, at present, eight grand-children, and eleven great-grandchildren. Since October 4, 1998, he has been the Pastor of the Bible For Today Baptist Church in Collingswood, New Jersey.

Order Blank (p. 1)

Name:_____

Address:_____

City & State:_____Zip:_____

Credit Card #:_____Expires:_____

Latest Books

[ ] Send The Fifth 200 Questions Answered By Dr. D. A. Waite
(150 pp. perfect bound $15.00 + $7.00 S&H)
[ ] Send *The Fourth 200 Questions Answered* By Dr. D. A. Waite
(168 pp. perfect bound $15.00 + $7.00 S&H)
[ ] Send *The Third 200 Questions Answered* By Dr. D. A. Waite
(180 pp. perfect bound $15.00 + $7.00 S&H)
[ ] Send *The Second 200 Questions Answered* By Dr. D. A. Waite
(178 pp. perfect bound $15.00 + $7.00 S&H)
[ ] Send *The First 200 Questions Answered By Dr. D. A. Waite*
(184 pp. perfect bound $12.00 + $7.00 S&H)
[ ] Send *A Critical Answer to James Price's King James Only-ism* By Pastor D. A. Waite, 184pp, perfect bound ($11+$7 S&H)
[ ] Send *The KJB's Superior Hebrew & Greek Words* by Pastor
D. A. Waite, 104 pp., perfect bound ($10+$7 S&H)
[ ] Send *Soulwinning's Versions-Perversions* by Pastor D. A.
Waite, booklet, 28 pp. ($6+$5 S&H) fully indexed
[ ] Send *2 Timothy--Preaching Verse by Verse*, by Pastor D. A.
Waite, 250 pages, perfect bound ($11+$7 S&H) fully indexed.
[ ] Send *A Critical Answer to God's Word Preserved* by Pastor D.
A. Waite, 192 pp. perfect bound ($11.00+$7.00 S&H)
[ ] Send *Daily Bible Blessings* By Yvonne Waite ($20.00+$8 S&H
[ ] Send *Revelation–Preaching Verse By Verse* By Dr. D. A. Waite
($50+$10 S&H--1030 pages.
[ ] Send *The Occult Connections of Gail Riplinger* by Dr. Phil
Stringer ($12.00 + $7.00 S&H).

The Most Recently Published Books

Send or Call Orders to:
THE BIBLE FOR TODAY
900 Park Ave., Collingswood, NJ 08108
Phone: 856-854-4452; FAX:--2464; Orders: 1-800 JOHN 10:9
E-Mail Orders: BFT@BibleForToday.org; Credit Cards OK

Order Blank (p. 2)

Name:_____

Address:_____

City & State:_____Zip:_____

Credit Card #:_____Expires:_____
[ ] Send *A WARNING!! On Gail Riplinger's KJB & Multiple Inspiration HERESY*,133 pp. by Pastor DAW ($12+$7S&H)
[ ] Send *Who Is Gail Riplinger?* 146 pp. by Aleithia O'Brien ($12.00 + $7.00)
[ ] *The Messianic Claims Of Gail A. Riplinger*, By Dr. Phil Stringer, 108 pp., perfect bound ($12.00 + $7.00 S&H)
[ ] Send Husband-Loving Lessons, by Yvonne S. Waite; $25 + $7.00 S&H A very valuable marriage manual
[ ] Send *8,000 Differences Between Textus Receptus & Critical Text* by Dr.J.A. Moorman, 544 pp., hd.back ($20+$7 S&H)
[ ] *Early Manuscripts, Church Fathers, & the Authorized Version* by Dr. Jack Moorman, $20+$7 S&H. Hardback
[ ] Send *The LIE That Changed the Modern World* by Dr. H. D. Williams ($16+$7 S&H) Hardback book
[ ] Send *With Tears in My Heart* by Gertrude G. Sanborn. Hardback 414 pp. ($25+$7 S&H) 400 Christian Poems
Preaching Verse by Verse Books
[ ] Send *2 Timothy--Preaching Verse by Verse*, by Pastor D. A. Waite, 250 pages, hardback ($11+$7 S&H) fully indexed.
[ ] Send *1 Timothy--Preaching Verse by Verse*, by Pastor D. A.Waite, 288 pages, hardback ($14+$7 S&H) fully indexed.
More Preaching Verse by Verse Books
[ ] Send *Romans--Preaching Verse by Verse* by Pastor D. A. Waite 736 pp. Hardback ($25+$7 S&H) fully indexed
[ ] Send *Colossians & Philemon--Preaching Verse by Verse* by Pastor D. A. Waite ($12+$7 S&H) hardback, 240 pages
[ ] Send *First Peter--Preaching Verse By Verse* by Pastor D. A. Waite ($10+$7 S&H) hardback, 176 pages
Send or Call Orders to:
THE BIBLE FOR TODAY
900 Park Ave., Collingswood, NJ 08108
Phone: 856-854-4452; FAX:--2464; Orders: 1-800 JOHN 10:9

Order Blank (p. 3)

Name:_____

Address:_____

City & State:_____Zip:_____

Credit Card #:_____Expires:_____
[ ] Send *Philippians--Preaching Verse by Verse* by Pastor D.
    A. Waite ($10+$7 S&H) hardback, 176 pages
[ ] Send *Ephesians--Preaching Verse by Verse* by Pastor D. A.
    Waite ($12+$7 S&H) hardback, 224 pages
[ ] Send *Galatians--Preaching Verse By Verse* by Pastor D. A.
    Waite ($13+$7 S&H) hardback, 216 pages
Books on Bible Texts & Translations
[ ] Send *Defending the King James Bible* by DAW ($12+$7
    S&H) A hardback book, indexed with study questions
[ ] Send *BJU's Errors on Bible Preservation* by Dr. D. A.
    Waite, 110 pages, paperback ($8+$7 S&H) fully indexed
[ ] Send *Fundamentalist Deception on Bible Preservation* by
    Dr.Waite, ($8+$4 S&H), paperback, fully indexed
[ ] Send *Fundamentalist MIS-INFORMATION on Bible Ver-*
    sions by Dr. Waite ($7+$5 S&H) perfect bound, 136 pages
[ ] Send *Fundamentalist Distortions on Bible Versions* by
    Dr.Waite ($7+$4 S&H) A perfect bound book, 80 pages
[ ] Send *Fuzzy Facts From Fundamentalists* by Dr. D. A.
    Waite ($8.00 + $7.00 S&H)
More Books on Bible Texts & Translations
[ ] Send *Foes of the King James Bible Refuted* by DAW ($9
    +$7 S&H) A perfect bound book, 164 pages in length
[ ] Send *Central Seminary Refuted on Bible Versions* by Dr.
    Waite ($10+$7 S&H) A perfect bound book, 184 pages
[ ] Send *The Case for the King James Bible* by DAW ($8
    +$5 S&H) A perfect bound book, 112 pages in length
[ ] Send *Theological Heresies of Westcott and Hort* by Dr. D.
    A. Waite, ($8+$5 S&H) A printed booklet
Send or Call Orders to:
THE BIBLE FOR TODAY
900 Park Ave., Collingswood, NJ 08108
Phone: 856-854-4452; FAX:--2464; Orders: 1-800 JOHN 10:9
E-Mail Orders: BFT@BibleForToday.org; Credit Cards OK

Order Blank (p. 4)

Name:_____

Address:_____

City & State:_____Zip:_____

Credit Card #:_____Expires:_____
[ ] Send *Westcott's Denial of Resurrection*, Dr. Waite ($8+$5)
[ ] Send *Four Reasons for Defending KJB* by DAW ($4+$3)
More Books on Texts & Translations
[ ] Send *Holes in the Holman Christian Standard Bible* by Dr. Waite ($6+$4 S&H) A printed booklet, 40 pages
[ ] Send *Contemporary Eng. Version Exposed*, DAW ($6+$4)
[ ] Send *NIV Inclusive Language Exposed* by DAW ($7+$5)
[ ] Send *24 Hours of KJB Seminar* (4 DVD's)by DAW($50.00)
 + $10.00 S&H
Books By Dr. Jack Moorman
[ ] Send *Manuscript Digest of the N.T.* (721 pp.) By Dr. Jack Moorman, copy-machine bound ($50+$10.00 S&H)
[ ] *Early Manuscripts, Church Fathers, & the Authorized Version* by Dr. Jack Moorman, $20+$7 S&H. Hardback
[ ] Send *Forever Settled--Bible Documents & History Survey* by Dr. Jack Moorman, $20+$7 S&H. Hardback book
[ ] Send *When the KJB Departs from the So-Called "Majority Text"* By Dr. Jack Moorman ($17.00 + $7.00 S&H)
More Books By Dr. Jack Moorman
[ ] Send *Missing in Modern Bibles--Nestle/Aland/NIV Errors* by Dr. Jack Moorman, $8+$7 S&H
[ ] Send *The Doctrinal Heart of the Bible--Removed from Modern Versions* by Dr. Jack Moorman, VCR, $15 +$7 S&H
[ ] Send *Modern Bibles--The Dark Secret* by Dr. Jack Moorman, $5+$4 S&H
[ ] Send *Samuel P. Tregelles--The Man Who Made the Critical Text Acceptable to Bible Believers* by Dr. Moorman ($5+$3)
Send or Call Orders to:
THE BIBLE FOR TODAY
900 Park Ave., Collingswood, NJ 08108
Phone: 856-854-4452; FAX:--2464; Orders: 1-800 JOHN 10:9
E-Mail Orders: BFT@BibleForToday.org; Credit Cards OK

Order Blank (p. 5)

Name:_____

Address:_____

City & State:_____Zip:_____

Credit Card #:_____Expires:_____
[ ] Send *8,000 Differences Between TR & CT* by Dr. Jack
Moorman [$20 + $7.00 S&H] a hardback book
Books By or About Dean Burgon
[ ] Send *The Revision Revised* by Dean Burgon ($25 + $7
S&H) A hardback book, 640 pages in length
[ ] Send *356 Doctrinal Errors in the NIV & Other Modern
Versions*, 100-large-pages, $10.00+$7 S&H
[ ] Send *The Last 12 verses of Mark* by Dean Burgon ($15+$7
S&H) A hardback book 400 pages
[ ] Send *The Traditional Text* hardback by Burgon ($15+$5
S&H) A hardback book, 384 pages in length
[ ] Send *Causes of Corruption* by Burgon ($16+$5 S&H)
A hardback book, 360 pages in length
More Books By or About Dean Burgon
[ ] Send *Inspiration and Interpretation*, Dean Burgon ($25+$7
S&H) A hardback book, 610 pages in length
[ ] Send *Burgon's Warnings on Revision* by DAW ($7+$5
S&H) A perfect bound book, 120 pages in length
[ ] Send *Westcott & Hort's Greek Text & Theory Refuted by
Burgon's Revision Revised--Summarized* by Dr. D. A.
Waite ($7.00+$5 S&H), 120 pages, perfect bound
[ ] Send *Dean Burgon's Confidence in KJB* by DAW ($5+$4)
[ ] Send *Vindicating Mark 16:9-20* by Dr. Waite ($5+$4S&H)
[ ] Send *Summary of Traditional Text* by Dr. Waite ($5 +$4)
[ ] Send *Summary of Causes of Corruption*, DAW ($5+$4)
[ ] Send *Summary of Inspiration* by Dr. Waite ($5+$4 S&H)

Send or Call Orders to:
THE BIBLE FOR TODAY
900 Park Ave., Collingswood, NJ 08108
Phone: 856-854-4452; FAX:--2464; Orders: 1-800 JOHN 10:9
E-Mail Orders: BFT@BibleForToday.org; Credit Cards OK

Order Blank (p. 6)

Name:_____

Address:_____

City & State:_____Zip:_____

Credit Card #:_____Expires:_____

More Books by Dr. D. A. Waite

[ ] Send *Making Marriage Melodious* by Pastor D. A. Waite
($7+$5 S&H), perfect bound, 112 pages

Books by D. A. Waite, Jr.

[ ] Send *Readability of A.V. (KJB)* by D. A. Waite, Jr. ($7+$4)
[ ] Send *4,114 Definitions from the Defined King James Bible*
by D. A. Waite, Jr. ($7.00+$5.00 S&H)
[ ] Send *The Doctored New Testament* by D. A. Waite, Jr.
($25+$7.00 S&H) Greek MSS differences shown, hardback
[ ] Send *Defined King James Bible* lg. prt. leather ($40+$10)
[ ] Send *Defined King James Bible* med. leather $35+$8.50)

Miscellaneous Authors

[ ] Send *The Attack on the Canon of Scripture* by Dr. H. D.
Williams, perfect bound ($15.00 + $7.00 S&H)
[ ] Send *Word-For-Word Translating of The Received Texts* by
Dr. H. D. Williams, 288 pages, paperback ($10+$7 S&H).
[ ] Send *Guide to Textual Criticism* by Edward Miller
($11+$7 S&H) a hardback book
[ ] Send *Scrivener's Greek New Testament Underlying the
King James Bible*, hardback, ($14 + $7 S&H)
[ ] Send *Scrivener's Annotated Greek New Testament*, by Dr.
Frederick Scrivener: Hardback--($35+$7 S&H);
Genuine Leather--($45+$7 S&H)
[ ] Send *Why Not the King James Bible?--An Answer to James
White's KJVO Book* by Dr. K. D. DiVietro, $10+$7 S&H
[ ] Send Brochure #1: "Over *1000 Titles Defending the
KJB/TR*" No Charge

Send or Call Orders to:
THE BIBLE FOR TODAY
900 Park Ave., Collingswood, NJ 08108
Phone: 856-854-4452; FAX:--2464; Orders: 1-800 JOHN 10:9
E-Mail Orders: BFT@BibleForToday.org; Credit Cards OK

The Defined
𝕶𝖎𝖓𝖌 𝕵𝖆𝖒𝖊𝖘 𝕭𝖎𝖇𝖑𝖊
Uncommon Words Defined Accurately

I. Deluxe Genuine Leather

✦𝕷𝖆𝖗𝖌𝖊 𝕻𝖗𝖎𝖓𝖙--𝕭𝖑𝖆𝖈𝖐 𝖔𝖗 𝕭𝖚𝖗𝖌𝖚𝖓𝖉𝖞✦

1 for $40.00+$10.00 S&H
✦Case of 12 for $360.00✦
$30.00 each+$35 S&H

✦𝕸𝖊𝖉𝖎𝖚𝖒 𝕻𝖗𝖎𝖓𝖙--𝕭𝖑𝖆𝖈𝖐 𝖔𝖗 𝕭𝖚𝖗𝖌𝖚𝖓𝖉𝖞 ✦

1 for $35.00+$8.50 S&H
✦Case of 12 for $300.00✦
$25.00 each+$25 S&H

II. Deluxe Hardback Editions

1 for $20.00+$10.00 S&H (Large Print)
✦Case of 12 for $180.00✦
$15.00 each+$35 S&H (Large Print)
1 for $15.00+$7.50 S&H (Medium Print)
✦Case of 12 for $120.00✦
$10.00 each+$25 S&H (Medium Print)

Order Phone: 1-800-JOHN 10:9
Credit Cards Welcomed

Pastor D. A. Waite, Th.D., Ph.D.

200 More Questions

- **The Reason For This Book.** I have put into print both The First, Second, Third and Fourth 200 Questions and Answers (BFT #3309, #3473, #3482, & #3494), but I still have more questions that have been asked me through the years. This book takes up questions ##801 to 1000. Some of these might be your questions as well.

- **The Goal of This Book.** The goal of this Fifth 200 Questions and Answers is similar to that of the First, Second, Third, and Fourth 200 Questions. I want to give our readers an understanding of where I stand on many additional controversial issues.

- **The Name of This Book.** The title of the book, The Fifth 200 Questions Answered by Dr. D. A. Waite, bears witness to the fact that there was a First , Second, Third, & Fourth 200 Questions. It implied that there could one day be a Fifth 200 Questions. This has come to pass now.

- **The Usefulness of This Book.** The author of a book can never predict whether or not his book is either useful or not useful. This depends on the opinions and needs of the readers. Are they fully informed on the topics that are discussed? Do they know the answers? If they do not know the answers, do they really want to find them out? It seems that many people are not concerned with Biblical subjects. The tool that makes this book useful to those who read it is the lengthy Index of Words and Phrases. You will find this Index very helpful to you.

www.BibleForToday.org

BFT 4014 BK   ISBN #978-1-56848-085-5

www.ingramcontent.com/pod-product-compliance
Lightning Source LLC
Chambersburg PA
CBHW071431090426
42737CB00011B/1627